OECD

REVIEWS OF NATIONAL POLICIES FOR EDUCATION

NORWAY

ORGANISATION FOR ECONOMIC CO-OPERATION AND DEVELOPMENT

Pursuant to article 1 of the Convention signed in Paris on 14th December 1960, and which came into force on 30th September 1961, the Organisation for Economic Co-operation and Development (OECD) shall promote policies designed:

- to achieve the highest sustainable economic growth and employment and a rising standard of living in Member countries, while maintaining financial stability, and thus to contribute to the development of the world economy;
- to contribute to sound economic expansion in Member as well as non-member countries in the process of economic development; and
- to contribute to the expansion of world trade on a multilateral, non-discriminatory basis in accordance with international obligations.

The original Member countries of the OECD are Austria, Belgium, Canada, Denmark, France, the Federal Republic of Germany, Greece, Iceland, Ireland, Italy, Luxembourg, the Netherlands, Norway, Portugal, Spain, Sweden, Switzerland, Turkey, the United Kingdom and the United States. The following countries acceded subsequently through accession at the dates indicated hereafter: Japan (28th April 1964), Finland (28th January 1969), Australia (7th June 1971) and New Zealand (29th May 1973).

The Socialist Federal Republic of Yugoslavia takes part in some of the work of the OECD (agreement of 28th October 1961).

Publié en français sous le titre:

EXAMENS DES POLITIQUES NATIONALES D'ÉDUCATION : NORVÈGE

© OECD, 1990
Application for permission to reproduce or translate all or part of this publication should be made to:
Head of Publications Service, OECD
2, rue André-Pascal, 75775 PARIS CEDEX 16, France.

Norway first invited a team of examiners thirteen years ago. For this review, the examiners were asked to perform an assessment of the education system of the same scope and range as that conducted in 1974; the main themes being: governance and policy-making, resource constraints and efficiency, school systems, higher education, equality and teacher policies.

Their report begins by singling out essential features of Norway that affect the provision of education, especially the impact of geography, the tradition of government, the absence of social classes, the status of education and, of course, the major changes in the economy caused by national and international oil policies.

On the governance and policy-making of the education system, the examiners perceived several priority needs relating to the strong Norwegian movement towards decentralisation. They underline the fact that a redistribution of power in favour of regional and local communities must be accompanied by a new clarification of the functions of governance and decision-making at each level of the administration.

It is believed that the authorities cannot easily monitor and evaluate the school system with the current governing structures. These could be either too numerous or traditional at central level, while some intermediary levels are not yet equipped for specific decision-making or thorough follow-up of educational outcomes. While approving healthy developments of the decentralisation process, the examiners suggest devising effective instruments for monitoring the system at its different levels.

Because of the new economic context characterised by tight public sector spending, the examiners express some doubts about the possibility of continuing generous support to small educational units, as was previously the case. In longer-term perspectives, they even advocate some rationalisation of the current network of educational institutions, especially in higher education. They also indicate that an improvement of basic data and research could help in using more efficiently the resources presently allocated to the whole system.

On basic education, they note with approval the major move made in the field of curriculum with the 1977 *Mønsterplan*, characterised by an important devolution of decision, within a national frame, to individual schools and their staff. Recalling that to be successful such a school-based curriculum development must be supported by self-improvement projects, strong leadership based on the consensus of the main partners (especially parents) and higher qualifications amongst school staff, they very much agree with some strategic measures already implemented.

The examiners also praise the comprehensive programme at senior secondary school. They nevertheless think that the multiple objectives of such an ambitious plan call for a regular increase of human and material resources. They also consider that the current updating process should be aimed at securing strong support from pupils and other groups as employers.

On higher education, the examiners focus on the the need to remandate higher education and particularly the universities. If the rapid development of the regional colleges has met specific needs, it now seems necessary to consider how to relate the different parts of higher education into an integrated system. Various research activities of a fundamental or applied nature must also be looked at in a more coherent and collaborative way between the universities, the regional colleges and the other independent research institutes. They ask if a social contract with higher education would not be able to guarantee greater degree of budgetary certainty and freedom in managing these institutions. In relation with the needs of the labour market, the examiners recommend that plans be designed to ensure that the ablest students undertake longer courses offered by the universities and that joint involvement between educational institutions and enterprises help in eliminating shortages of highly-qualified manpower in strategic fields such as engineering or teaching.

Such co-operation and dialogue between the education systems and the outside world is also advocated at other levels of the system, especially senior secondary school and adult education.

Recalling the Norwegian tradition of equality and the great steps taken to achieve it, the examiners express the view that in the current context of rapid socio-technical changes, equality of opportunity cannot be separated from the quality of schooling. To this end, there is a call to increase individualisation of needs assessment and of teaching and learning processes. In this, the teaching profession has a key role and it needs to be fully equipped for such difficult tasks. Teacher recruitment, partly determined by the status of the teacher in society, and continuing teacher training will still be a priority policy area in the near future.

A record of the review meeting, which contains full replies to the examiners' questions, constitutes Part Two of this volume and Part Three comprises a summary of the Norwegian authorities' Background Report.

TABLE OF CONTENTS

The OECD Examiners and the Norwegian Delegation 8

Part One
THE EXAMINERS' REPORT

I.	Introduction	9
II.	The Norwegian Context	13
III.	Policy Changes and Objectives in Schools	23
IV.	Policy Changes and Objectives in Higher and Adult Education	33
V.	Structure and Governance	45
VI.	Critical Perspectives and Proposals	53

Part Two
RECORD OF THE REVIEW MEETING
Paris, 28 May 1988

	Opening Address by the Norwegian Minister of Church and Education	65
I.	Resource Constraints on the Achievement of Objectives	68
II.	The Role of Central Government and the Local Authorities	70
III.	Data and Evaluation, and their Connection with Decentralisation	72
IV.	Higher Education	76
V.	Education and the Labour Market	78
VI.	The Upper Secondary School	79
VII.	Some General Points	79
VIII.	Teacher Education	81
	Concluding Remarks	82

Part Three
NATIONAL POLICIES FOR EDUCATION IN NORWAY
Summary of the Background Report
prepared by the Royal Ministry of Cultural and Scientific Affairs
and the Royal Ministry of Church and Education
Oslo, 1988

I.	Country and people	85
II.	The Education System	87
III.	Special Items	91
IV.	Some Key Issues	95

Also available

REVIEWS OF NATIONAL POLICIES FOR EDUCATION:

ICELAND (1987)
(91 87 01 1) ISBN 92-64-13028-4, 98 pp.   £8.00   US$17.00   FF80   DM35

ITALY. Educational Reforms (1985)
(91 85 01 1) ISBN 92-64-12702-X, 112 pp.   £7.50   US$15.00   FF75   DM33

NEW ZEALAND (1983)
(91 83 04 1) ISBN 92-64-12477-2, 140 pp.   £6.60   US$13.00   FF66   DM30

PORTUGAL (1984)
(91 84 01 1) ISBN 92-64-12568-X, 110 pp.   £6.00   US$12.00   FF60   DM16

SPAIN (1987)
(91 87 01 1) ISBN 92-64-12902-2, 108 pp.   £9.00   US$18.00   FF90   DM40

SWEDEN. Educational Reforms (1981)
(91 81 03 1) ISBN 92-64-12150-1, 108 pp.   £3.20   US$8.00   FF32   DM16

TURKEY (1989)
(91 89 01 1) ISBN 92-64-13207-4, 114 pp.   £11.50   US$20.00   FF95   DM39

YUGOSLAVIA (1982)
(91 82 01 1) ISBN 92-64-12270-2, 152 pp.   £4.30   US$9.50   FF43   DM22

SCHOOLS AND QUALITY: An International Report (1989)
(91 89 02 1) ISBN 92-64-13254-6, 156 pages   £11.50   US$20.00   FF95   DM39

Prices charged at the OECD Bookshop.

The OECD CATALOGUE OF PUBLICATIONS and supplements will be sent free of charge on request addressed either to OECD Publications Service, 2, rue André-Pascal, 75775 PARIS CEDEX 16, or to the OECD Distributor in your country.

Part One

THE EXAMINERS' REPORT

THE OECD EXAMINERS

Mr. M. O'DONOGHUE	Trinity College, Dublin, Ireland
Mr. M. KOGAN (Rapporteur)	Brunel University, Uxbridge, United Kingdom
Mr. U. LUNDGREN	Institute of Education, Stockholm, Sweden

THE NORWEGIAN DELEGATION

Mr. Halvard BAKKE	Minister of Cultural and Scientific Affairs
Mrs. Kirsti KOLLE GRØNDAHL	Minister of Church and Education
Mrs. Elisabeth WALAAS	Personal Advisor, Ministry of Cultural and Scientific Affairs
Mr. Morten LAUVBU	Personal Advisor, Ministry of Church and Education
Mr. Kjell EIDE	Director General, Ministry of Cultural and Scientific Affairs
Mr. Arve KJELBERG	Director General, Ministry of Cultural and Scientific Affairs
Mr. Oddvar VORMELAND	Director General, Ministry of Church and Education
Mr. Jon Chr. LØKEN	Special Counsellor, Ministry of Church and Education
Mr. Per Kr. PEDERSEN	Minister Counsellor, Acting Permanent Representative
Mr. Knut Eggum JOHANSEN	Special Advisor, Permanent Delegation to the OECD

I
INTRODUCTION

Terms of reference and the Norwegian invitation

Of all the OECD countries, Norway displays tension and interplay between traditional assumptions and modes of behaviour and a desire to transform society for the benefit of all of its citizens. That it largely reconciles the conflict between historically endorsed values and social progress derives from the infusion of the Norwegian ethic with notions of respect for the individual, for the rights of local groups and for the rule of law. In the course of our examination, we observed the power of tradition operating in a country where, since the previous OECD review in 1974, there have been radical changes in the education system itself and in its economic and social background.

In order to assess these movements of policy and practice the Norwegian government asked the OECD to perform an assessment of the education system of the same scope and range as that conducted thirteen years before. The review visitation occupied two weeks in November 1987.

We gratefully acknowledge the assistance and kind hospitality accorded to us by our hosts. The Royal Ministries of Cultural and Scientific Affairs and of Church and Education helped us greatly in producing for our use the *Background Report on Norway: OECD Reviews of National Policies for Education*, 1987. In this document, the Norwegian authorities fully and frankly outlined both their achievements and their problems, their causes for pride and the uncertainties which still remain in the formulation and implementation of educational policy.

The programme of visits and work

During our visit, and perhaps as a demonstration of their own ethic, our Norwegian hosts worked us hard. We spent a great deal of time with the national bodies; these included the two ministries responsible for education, as well as representatives of students, teachers, local authorities, adult education organisations, the advisory councils, the trade unions and employers. We were privileged to meet members of the Parliamentary Committee on Education. We visited schools, colleges, and universities in the areas of Oslo, Bergen and Bodo, a region which would have been described by a previous Minister of Education (see the 1974 review) as being "at the periphery of the periphery". Throughout all of our visits, and in all of our encounters we were treated with warmth, courtesy, openness and frankness. It is not possible to name all of those who received us. In particular we must thank officials of the two Ministries who did so much to make our visit successful and happy, and most of all Mr. Jon Løken, the Deputy Director General of the Royal Ministry of Church and Education who collated our programme and was our expert guide for most of our visits. Mr. K. Eide of the Ministry of Cultural and Scientific Affairs contributed significantly to the preparation and documentation for the exercise.

Main changes since 1974

The examiners had access to a series of expert OECD and other reports directly relevant to our terms of reference.

Half a generation ago, in 1974, the Norwegian education system was reviewed, and the foresight of our predecessors leaps from every page of their report. Much of what they say about the background factors remains relevant today. Perhaps the largest changes are those brought about by the exploitation of the oil reserves. But even that scene is changing: we visited when uncertainties about the economy were becoming prominent and the resources available for the public sector, including education, more contestable.

Norway, too, as do other European countries, has a population which is both growing at a slower rate and ageing. These demographic trends will affect educational policy in several ways. As Ministers told us, the economy will need to get good value for the education given to young people if it is to sustain the balance between producers and recipients from the economy. An ageing population, the majority of whom were brought up in a period of relatively frugal educational opportunity, will be eligible for continuing education in all of its manifestations. Whilst the institutions and local authorities, already catering for small numbers, will find their school-age clientele thinning out, the educational and social demands on the system will become more various and complex.

So our visit was paid at a time to take stock of great achievements but also when Norwegian policy-makers face a stiff working agenda.

Since 1974 there has been a great increase in access to higher education and the majority, some 90 per cent of young people, enter the upper secondary school and 70 per cent of the 16 to 18 age group remain in education. Secondary education has broken away from its selective past towards a system of comprehensive education. In particular, upper secondary education has been thoroughly reorganised following the Act of 1974 which came into force in 1976. There have been radical changes, some yet to be fully digested, resulting from the decentralisation of power from the central ministries to local authorities and higher education institutions. The main reform of special education dates back to 1974 and its extension to upper secondary education is now being implemented. Since 1974 the arrival of immigrant groups has presented new challenges and opportunities to the schools.

When our predecessors visited Norway, the authorities identified four major problem areas: participation in policy-making; equality; integration of post-compulsory education, and innovation and planning policies. These issues remain salient although so much effort has been put into dealing with them. Our predecessors came at a time of considerable emphasis on new policy input. Our analysis comes at a time when those inputs could have been expected to be converted into outcomes ready for national and international evaluation.

Other OECD reports

Apart from the report of the 1974 review of national policy for education, we benefited from OECD's *Review of National Science Policy* (1975) and the *Economic Survey 1986/87* (1987). Whilst the Economic Survey is virtually silent on the role of training or education in the Norwegian economy, the *Review of Science Policy* deals with many issues of relevance to higher education policy. The reviewers noted that there were problems in decision-making, in the resources available to the university research system, and structural problems, including the size and number of institutions, the disciplinary set-up and the regional distribution of institutions and the exchange of information. We shall be returning to the points made in that interesting and valuable report later in our own review. We have also consulted the CERI Examiners' Report, *The Introduction of Computers in Schools: The Norwegian Experience* (1987), a report of visitors appraising *Integration of Handicapped Pupils in Compulsory Education in Norway* (1983), and a report commissioned by OECD/CERI on issues of secondary teacher training in Norway by Mrs. A. L. Hostmark-Tarrou.

II

THE NORWEGIAN CONTEXT

The inheritance of history

In some senses Norway is both an old and a new society. It is old in that it has a long tradition of national unity. It is new in that it had to build itself as a nation in the nineteenth century. The formation of modern Norwegian society and the state is to be linked with its liberation from Denmark and Sweden, the political and constitutional changes of 1814, and the dissolution of union with Sweden in 1905. But forming the national identity began in the eighteenth century when the intellectual elite played an important role in the articulation of a nationality. A key element was conflict about language. The work by Aasen in the 1850s to build up a "country language", based mainly on the dialects of the western parts of Norway, as opposed to the "city language" influenced by Danish, illustrates the continuity of these movements into the twentieth century. The existence of two variants of the language has had an impact on education; teachers must master both.

The struggle for independence from Sweden helped form a modern national identity. The German occupation of Norway during the Second World War and active Norwegian resistance reinforced national pride. The National Day -17 May - is perhaps Norway's most important holiday during which the Nordic temperament expresses itself in somewhat exotic forms. It is the day of both the constitution of Eidsvold (1814), and the day of liberation (the German army surrendered on 7 May 1945). The sense of being a nation is paralleled by a strong sense of local identity which is an important feature of the cultural landscape.

The impact of geography on politics and structure

Norway has a population of just over four million people but possesses one of the largest and longest land masses in Europe. It covers nearly 325 thousand square kilometers. Historically communications have been by water. As a result its parts have been isolated from each other and have developed local traditions and a sense of community. It is on this local identity that a sense of a modern nation has been built. Government by Denmark and the union with Sweden must have strengthened the sense of distance between the centre and the periphery, and the distance between city and country. This is seen also in the development of the education system.

Whilst its culture and traditions are remarkably homogeneous, geography affects both politics and the structure of education, particularly given the long distances over which communications and relationships are sustained. There is a fierce pride in geographical origins and a belief in the freedom of local people to live and work in their own ways. In the words of Dr. Ingrid Eide, leader of the Norwegian delegation in the 1974 review, "There is political consensus that the country must continue to have a population living a dispersed pattern, and that we must pay for it and construct for it. We do not want an excessive amount of mobility, either geographically or in other terms." A centrally organised school system was an important mechanism in making a cohesive nation out of a dispersed population.

Therefore, whilst Norwegian education has always been centrally controlled, national policies have had to take account of the power of the localities. The same diffusion of power permeates national policy-making which is corporatist; policies have to be negotiated with a large number of political parties and interest groups which themselves connect strongly with local interests. As a result, central ministries hold the ring between the "real" forces in the field and exercise power carefully. Policies have at the same time, and perhaps to offset differences, been incorporated and implemented through formal rules and financial regulations. This has not allowed government to fully exercise the power to rule and to plan in a strong or active sense. For example, deference to local wishes which has gone along with this central regulation of detail and the control of budgets has resulted in a prolific distribution of power to a large number of local authorities, working on two levels, and in the generous distribution of higher education to a large number of regional and local institutions. As an example of the determined distribution of power and of resources the Norwegian example is admirable. As an example of a modern state facing the problems of equality of provision and of educational standards, it raises problems. These are noted in the Background Report which expresses the determination to consolidate some institutions and not allow the proliferation of new ones.

The changing economy

The Norwegian economy has developed rapidly for almost two decades, largely due to the impetus from the oil industry. Since the first oil shock of 1973, GDP growth has been double the average of other OECD European Members, and employment has grown strongly to produce one of the lowest unemployment rates. At the same time, inflationary pressures have not been sufficiently under control. Although the inflation rate has declined it has been signficantly higher than the OECD average; prices rose by 70 per cent in the 1979 to 1985 period.

The collapse of oil prices in 1986 marked a turning point; export earnings were reduced by more than 15 per cent, and there was a loss of about 10 per cent in real income. The current balance of payments moved sharply into deficit. It still took time to arrest the growth in private consumption which went up 17 per cent in 1985 and 1986. There is little evidence of any early return to the high oil prices of the 1979-1985 period; significant adjustment in the pattern of economy activity will, therefore, be needed. It may then be only a matter of time before resources must be moved to the "traded" section to expand exports and reduce imports. The corollary will be that fewer resources are available for domestic production and consumption. This switch in activity is likely to have noticeable effects in the public sector whose budgets correspond to about 45 per cent of GNP although this includes a high complement of transfer payments. Lower oil prices are resulting in sharp declines in oil tax revenues. Since other taxes are already high by international standards, the presumption must be that adjustment in the public sector will take the form of curbs on spending. The implications for the educational sector are clear. In 1986 public expenditure on education took about 5.8 per cent of the GNP, compared with 6.2 per cent in 1973; it is expected to return to the 1973 level in 1987 and 1988. It will be difficult to achieve any further significant increase in the value of resources directed to educational activities. Instead the focus is more likely to be directed towards achieving greater efficiency in the use of whatever resources are available. This presumption is reinforced by consideration of demographic trends. In common with other European countries there has been a major decline in births. This has already led to shortfalls in the numbers of children at primary school level, and will affect the upper levels of education in the coming years. As the numbers of young people leaving education to enter the labour market begin to decline it may be expected that the pressures to use this scarce labour more effectively will intensify.

In such an environment the priority to be given to education will remain strong but it may be expected that the education system will need to adjust its operating patterns so as to minimise its use of scarce labour. The contribution of education and training to the Norwegian economy can be manifold. A systematic increase in the pool of qualified and highly qualified manpower could be achieved by avoiding wastage from education among adolescents. It could more purposively induce adults to qualify and to return for requalification through various schemes of adult education. The economy is likely to need to have a reservoir of well-qualified people in the appropriate range of sectors who can be utilised in employment of all kinds and firms of all sizes. Norway will need particularly to emphasize the training of specialists for the export industries. At the same time, education must not be restricted to technical training but also conceived as producing dynamic and innovative people able to contribute to an economy that must be diversified, modernised and productive.

Such developments would mark a change from the previous pattern of educational development where, as in other countries, improvements have taken the form of providing greater relative numbers of teachers to produce smaller class sizes. The challenge for the future is to develop other dimensions of quality in educational provision.

There could certainly be more joint involvement between education and production enterprises in tackling specific needs. In the course of our review we visited interesting examples of enterprises incorporating co-operation between, for example, a school of engineering and a salmon farm, and an upper secondary school and the training of aircraft mechanics. But such cases were not widespread. We could not form a judgement in the time available on the matter, but were told more than once that the educational sector is somewhat divorced from the activities of firms and the needs of the labour market. Employers felt, too, that the schools were not providing young people with the necessary basic skills in Norwegian and mathematics. At the same time, teaching methods were too traditional; there was too much rote learning and insufficient problem-solving. This created a lack of self-confidence in pupils. They were also worried about student preferences for shorter higher education courses. Employers naturally have specific training for short-term objectives. They also deplored the continued emphasis on the public sector. Of the 40 000 new jobs last year over half had gone to the public sector. In all they did not feel they had sufficient influence over teachers and local authorities. The decentralised teacher training system was also difficult to influence. They also felt that "the losers became teachers" because salary and status were too low, a perception not borne out by the facts. Students in teacher training colleges do in fact graduate from upper secondary schools with better average marks than those of university students.

There is reluctance to become too involved in research or other activities on behalf of firms because of the fear that this would weaken or debase the educational work of the institution. From the employers' perspective the educational sector is frequently viewed as providing courses and services based on the interests of staff or on their perceptions of what industry ought to want, rather than making serious efforts to come to grips with working situations and problems.

Such tensions and criticisms are not exclusive to Norway. But given the rapid change in the economic and demographic frame its education system has particularly difficult problems to face and opportunities to exploit.

The tradition of government

As noted, the tradition of government in Norway is an amalgam of deference to the centre, to the rule of Parliamentary democracy, and to the vigorous distribution of power to the localities. It is there that the politicians and the professionals, both administrative and in the schools, have a powerful hold over what is provided.

The issue of centralisation will recur several times in our report. We here briefly sketch the background and the main elements of it and leave to later sections some of the more detailed consequences.

The Norwegian education system has always been centralised, even though some decisions have been local, such as adjustments of school days to seasonal work, selection of teachers, the provision of classrooms. Educational development in Denmark provided the motive power for the earlier school traditions and demands for schooling. Those acts by a centralised government later proved necessary to secure the modern reform of education and to provide a system offering equal opportunities. A legal tradition was thus reinforced by new policy demands and the education system continued to be closely regulated. Even now, the establishment of university professors and readers has to be approved by the government. In resourcing education reform the government was well able to relate funding to national policies but operated through complicated administrative rules. At the same time, the transition from selection to a comprehensive school system, which was itself to be linked to further education for all, called for the reformulation of the national curriculum which had already existed for more than half a century. The prolongation of comprehensive education called for a new curriculum plan which was adopted in 1974. In 1987 the new *Mønsterplan* was primarily a revision of the 1974 plan.

Educational reform in the 1970s, therefore, depended upon legal, economic and ideological instruments for its central government. But now decentralisation is the consensually accepted policy. The infrastructure of the school system is thought to have been built up. There are strong political demands for more local control over the implementation of the main reforms.

Thus, in the 1980s the "frame laws" inaugurated in the early 1970s have been revised to allow for a transfer of funds from central to local government. From 1986, the earmarking of subsidies to the municipalities has disappeared and the local community can allocate money between services as it thinks fit. The consequences of this reform still remain to emerge. Opposition to the block or general grant rested on the fear that if local authorities were allowed to choose between spending on education and on such other services as health and care for the elderly, made more necessary by an ageing population, school services will be consolidated, at the expense of making them available at the local level.

The way in which curriculum policy has been developed provides a good example of the Norwegian mode of government. Comprehensive education has been compulsory since 1920. In 1974 the extension of schooling by two years which had already taken place was legally confirmed. This was reinforced by a renewal of the curriculum. The Council for Primary and Lower Secondary Education worked out proposals and sent them out for consideration. All teachers were able to read them, and almost all seemed to have done so. Some of the amendments were based on their responses and, after a change of government, were accepted by Parliament. To thus involve teachers, parents and politicians meant that they were more likely to be committed to the implementation of the new curriculum. Conflicts were, however, resolved, but at the expense of an increase in the level of abstraction in the policy statements.

Such a move away from the traditional mode of government promises to replace legal and financial prescriptions by the use of local initiative. But moving from a highly centralised to a more decentralised system makes it all the more difficult to formulate and realise policy.

As we will see later, the 1987 version of the *Mønsterplan* extends further the discretion of the school but still lays down quite a great deal of what they may and should do. Relationships with the universities are said, in the Background Report, to be relaxed, but complaints of restriction are still heard. The centre defers to decentralisation to the point that it does not have the capacity to know how the *Mønsterplan* is working in the schools, or the nature of the groups enjoying higher education in its different modes, or, for that matter, the true costs of education throughout the country.

The system is well under the control of democratic rule. Whilst we heard complaints about the existence of a "permanent government" of officials (a complaint made in every Parliamentary democracy, as is usual in the Nordic countries), members of the Storting, and its Education Committee have a definite role in educational policy-making at the centre. At the same time, regional policy on some issues seems to have a stronger impact than do the national party policies. Local educational influences operate at the centre on the officials responsible for planning policy. This local "profile" of Parliament emerges in policy form in, for example, the prolific distribution of centres of higher education.

A further ingredient is the fact that whilst Norwegian educational policy-making is anything but apolitical, there is a stubborn sub-stratum of law and regulation through which it operates. It was explained in the course of the 1974 examination how the respect for the rule of law went back a thousand years to the Vikings who believed that it was impossible to have a nation which was not governed by law. That admirable tradition dies hard. It can mean, however, that there may be no intermediate position between the formal expression of policies through laws and budgets and their informal refreshment and sustenance outside the legal frameworks, through dissemination of knowledge and example. Communication and information flows are secondary but vital aspects of the modern government of a service which must constantly refresh itself by observing the lessons of its own experiences.

The key problem concerns the role of the centre in a decentralised system which cherishes the fragmentation of power. Governments, whether wishing to cause major social change, or seeking to turn the clock back, cannot avoid corporatist dealings with interest groups. Negotiations with the trade unions, with employers, with the newly powerful local authorities and their associations, the student unions, the teacher unions are all part of the scene through which ministers and their officials must move to generate support and sustain change. None of this is bizarre or eccentric within the Western democratic setting. What is, however, missing is the belief that with decentralisation the centre should not abandon its role but must find a new one. When a society moves from obedience to rules it must move towards more normative means of ensuring the refreshment, statement and implementation of policies. This means, therefore, not simply the reduction of central machinery so much as thinking of it in terms of patterns of information, monitoring and the dissemination of good practice through which the centre gains in influence at the same time as it relinquishes its formal powers.

On this description of the political-economic development it is possible to identify the changes from the middle of the nineteenth century and onwards as the building of an infrastructure of supporting regional initiative, with state support and private economy. This solution was called by one of the leading politicians at the time – Schweigaard (1838-1899) – "a Norwegian peculiarity". At the end of the century the state became more active and took the role of co-ordinator. During the period after the war Norwegian society was built on a Nordic model, with a mixed economy and a strong public sector as the basis for a welfare society and with close relations between the State and the co-operative groups.

The welfare model, with its instruments for governing, developed during the 1950s and 1960s and with the discovery of oil in the North Sea it was elaborated. During the 1970s with lower oil prices there were changes in the realisation of the welfare programme.

Expectations of state support have grown and have been increasingly in imbalance with state-monitored resources. During our visit to Sulitjema – a remote area facing the closure of the main industry, mining – this was clearly visible. Whilst the welfare society was being built the State stimulated and helped to form co-operative groups in order to have centres with which it could negotiate. In a declining economy these organisations overcrowd policy formulation and block active policy-making. It is in this context that traditions are to be understood. National pride based on local traditions and culture creates tensions between the centre and the periphery. The State supports local initiative, enterprise and traditions but does not control from the centre the implementation of programmes. As we have seen, there is little possibility that the public sector can be increased. There is an overcrowded political arena. It is therefore not surprising that the centre finds an opportunity to reduce its own role so that it lays down guidelines and leaves the realisation of policy to local communities. But decentralisation creates the need for a reappraisal of instruments for governing and new structures for information and evaluation.

Norwegian classlessness

The class structure in Norway is also somewhat different from that of other countries. The country was late in being industrialised and in the concentration of capital. The class structure is as strongly affected by the geographical background as by the distribution of wealth. The Norwegians have had to work hard to survive and the opportunity for the leisurely life has never been there. Yet intellectuals have played an important part in the struggle for independence and the building of the nation. At the same time, Norwegian art, literature and science have been of international importance.

Even though the class structure is somewhat different from other industrialised societies, Norwegian social stratification is related to education which has contributed greatly to changes in the social structure in Norway.

One aspect of the issue of equality is educational policy for ethnic minorities. In the last OECD review of 1974, the examiners noted the homogeneity of the Norwegian society.

"Norway contains no significant ethnic or cultural minorities. The Sami minority, while increasingly important to Norwegian educational policy, is so remote from the centre and so small in relation to the population that it has not been a factor in defining Norwegians' sense of identity – only recently have the collections on Lappish culture moved from the Ethnographic Museum to the Museums of Norwegian Folklore. While this, obviously, is a potential difficulty in dealing with the Lapps' developing sense of cultural identity, the basic homogeneity of Norwegian society has certainly simplified the problems of social policy" (p. 11). This picture of a homogeneous country can still be painted with broad strokes. There has, however, been significant immigration since 1976. In 1983 2.4 per cent were immigrants. Of these 60 per cent were from North America or North Europe. But the number of immigrants increased. The number from Asia or Africa is now more or less the same as the Sami population. Within urban areas this immigration has consequences for education. It reinforces the goal of equal opportunity, and calls for economic support to education as well as new forms of organisation and didactics.

Educational traditions

As a consequence of the pietist movement in Denmark demands for schooling were formulated in 1739. In what was appropriately called the "Danish school", the demand was for three months between seven and twelve years. How much schooling in reality there was can be disputed. In the rural areas the schools were established in the nineteenth century. In cities the school system developed an upper secondary level aiming towards the education of civil servants. The first law of compulsory schooling came in 1827, but did no more than reflect the demands of 1739. In 1860, however, the compulsory school became a reality through a new law. The formats were quite different in the country (*allmugeskolen*) and the cities. In the latter a rather elaborated system was developed with middle school and upper secondary school, patterned after Germany. In the climate following the Second World War it was important to create a system giving equal opportunities irrespective of geographical location.

The modern school reforms were built up in three steps. First the compulsory school (*Grunnskole*) was reformed in 1969 when a nine-year compulsory school was formed. The comprehensive school was built in two stages: stage 1-6 (*barnesteget*) and stage 7-9 (*ungdomssteget*). The second step was the reform of the upper secondary school (*Videregaende skole*) which offered a wide range of lines and study courses lasting from one to three years and aiming at further education or a vocation.

The third step was the formation of the tertiary level. The University of Oslo was established in 1811; as the only university until 1948 it played an important role in the forming of a national intellectual elite, particularly in the education of state servants. The University of Bergen which was founded on the base of the Bergen Museum was the second university to be followed by the University in Trondheim. In order to stimulate development in the northern regions a fourth university in Tromsø was established in the beginning of the seventies. The University of Tromsø has special obligations to develop higher education and research in the northern part of Norway. But in the seventies higher education policy shifted. Once the University of Tromsø was founded resources were used to establish regional colleges throughout the country although we are informed that resources spent on establishing regional colleges have not blocked the further development of the university sector. The main purpose was to bring higher education to the regions and to adjust higher education to local demands. Education at the post-graduate levels and graduate programmes are mainly offered at the universities. The regional colleges are now established and seem to be well "cogged into" the local context. They serve local needs for education, but also local demands for research and development; the tendency is for regional colleges to become increasingly ambitious and to offer more advanced courses. One example is the regional college of Bodo now giving courses in management studies. In pace with the ambition to strengthen the educational programmes, research projects are allocated to the regional colleges and research programmes are developed.

Tradition and geography have thus formed a system in which equal opportunity in education has, within a pragmatic policy, focused on establishing an education system well distributed across the country. The ultimate aim has been to match institutions of education with the demography, geography and traditions of the country. The costs of this policy have been difficulty of governing an increasingly decentralised education system, gaining information about the effects of the system and its changes, and extensive expenditure.

The status of education in Norway

In the 1960s education enjoyed public support; it has always received great respect in Norway. But in the 1970s a great deal of attention was paid to the infrastructure needed to support the newly flourishing oil industry, for example roads on the west coast. Other services such as health began to clamour for attention. Now teachers feel that they lack adequate status and remuneration. There are 80 000 teachers organised in 13 unions and they figure within the general complications of public sector settlements. We were told that whilst teachers must shoulder a much wider range of tasks they feel they lack the facilities for them. For example, they have no offices from which to undertake pastoral work. The restrictions on their role are being removed but they are not being equipped physically or through training to carry the new burdens.

Teachers' salaries, as those of others in the public sector, have fallen behind the burgeoning private sector. Many countries find it difficult to attract teachers of certain specialist subjects but in Norway there is a more general problem associated with a general loss of status.

Given the perceptions of their status, teachers will find it more difficult to move from a limited perspective of their role, construed in terms of neatly parcelled proportions of a school day, towards a more generous and fully professional approach which often disregards the boundaries of set time limits and centrally prescribed curricula. It was not easy for us to see how to break this vicious circle and we are aware that its further discussion would lead us on to difficult and contested terrain.

As we write our report, the teachers' unions are in dispute with the government. We are not qualified to comment on issues of remuneration and conditions of service but we are struck by the extent to which burdens on the schools have become heavier in spite of increased teaching resources and reduced teaching obligations for individual teachers. Decentralisation ought to be an excellent opportunity for self-appraisal but that might be simply demoralising in the current context of uncertainty and of decreasing status. So many aspects of the whole education system come into play as one reflects upon the factors affecting the status of teachers. There are the issues of recruitment and training to which we return later in this report. There is the way in which teachers are located in different jobs and its relationship to levels of qualification. There are problems of establishing the appropriate balance between recruiting teachers at a rate that can be afforded and the pressure from the outside world with attractive salaries for less important work. There are the needs to strengthen training courses without further increasing the cost to the system.

Other indications of education's status is the relative lack of interest shown by young people in the pursuit of higher education for its own sake. The longer general courses of study, which are usually highly competed for in other countries, are held in less favour than shorter courses more generally directed to the job market. The labour market is tight and employers offer attractive salaries to young adults who have not sometimes completed their specialised studies.

III

POLICY CHANGES AND OBJECTIVES IN SCHOOLS

With these contextual matters in mind we turn to look more closely at the main features of the Norwegian system as seen through its institutions at the departmental levels and its governing structures.

The stages of schooling

In considering the organisation of schooling into its different stages, two conflicting principles can be observed. Young people ought to be allowed to develop at different times in the ways appropriate to the stage that they have reached. In particular, the imperatives that affect education for people about to enter the world of work should not dominate the education of the younger people. At the same time, however, connection and progression should be encouraged between the different stages.

The Norwegian school system is characterised by administrative divisions. The importance of the kindergarten is emphasized in relation to the large changes in the patterns of family life being experienced in Norway as in other countries. The kindergarten, although stated to be both educational and social in its objectives, is organised under the Ministry of Consumer Affairs and Administration and not the Ministry of Church and Education. Experiments in bringing it closer to primary education are being undertaken now. The government hopes to add 10 000 places each year until the year 2000; this target is thought to be difficult to achieve. At present, however, only 30 per cent of the eligible age group attend kindergartens and half of these are in private establishments. There is also an ambitious expansion programme for both kindergarten places and for teacher training to staff them. The direction of kindergarten and preschool education is not, however, without problems. General public criticisms of education arguing for more basic instruction has also launched a debate about strengthening the pedagogical programmes in preschools. The effects of various preschool organisations and programmes are being evaluated in order to broaden the decision basis for the expansion of preschool education.

The main system of schooling divides between the primary and lower secondary (sometimes known as the basic school) and the upper secondary stages. The primary school lasts from grades 1 to 6 and caters for children between seven and 13. It is often part of the same school as the lower secondary school which caters for grades 7 to 9 for children from 14 to 16 years. The upper secondary school, which recruits about 90 per cent of lower secondary school leavers, occupies grades 9 to 12 for young people of between 16 to 19 and incorporates the whole range of education and training from the general courses in the humanities, science and mathematics to schemes forming part of specific training for apprenticeships. The term "tertiary college" was applied to some of them during our visit. The provision of schooling in single schools for grades 1 to 9 is usually enforced by geographical considerations.

All schools, comprehensive and upper secondary, fall within the jurisdiction of the Ministry of Church and Education but the primary and lower secondary schools are the province of the municipal or community authorities whilst the upper secondary schools belong to the counties or regions. We were told how schools make efforts to ensure connection between the different stages. It seems unlikely, however, that local authorities can ensure that schools work together over the age divides; we have been told of cases where accommodation underused in one school, and under one local authority, could not be used by another overloaded school which was within the province of another authority.

It is never easy to bridge the gulf between stages: pupils from good primary schools notoriously regress on entry to those secondary schools where the educational emphasis is too often upon instrumental instruction for the older pupils. If they were, however, within the ambit of one local authority, at least the formal obstacles to collaboration would be removed.

New objectives for comprehensive schools and the 1987 Mønsterplan

The Norwegian word *Mønsterplan* literally means "pattern plan", and is not easily translated into the English term curriculum. The *Mønsterplan* is decided by the government, guided by discussion in Parliament. It lays down the general goals and the content of teaching for the comprehensive school system. It is thus one of the most important instruments for the central governing of education.

The *Mønsterplan* of 1987 has a different structure from the earlier one. It still states national goals for the education system but it is also adjusted to a more decentralised system. Within the frames given, each school is invited to form its local curriculum as a working plan. The working plan is an instrument for transforming the goals for the education system into concrete goals for the school. In the process of creating the working plan the schools are expected to plan their work more systematically than before in relation to available resources. In this way the *Mønsterplan* is intended to stimulate local educational planning and to renew pedagogical awareness of the relation between goals and methods.

This strategy calls for a new surge of resources for evaluation at the local level. If the working plan is to be an instrument for local school development, it has to be successively evaluated and revised. In this process the working plan also forms a basis for local development projects and in-service training of teachers. Its implementation would emphatically demand new competence in teachers' planning of the curriculum.

From a curriculum theory and an educational planning perspective the new *Mønsterplan* promises the use of curricula as instruments for governing. At the same time it creates consequences for the overall planning process and for the evaluation of the school system. In particular it raises the question: how can national goals for the compulsory school system be guaranteed within the framework of the *Mønsterplan*?

Our evaluation of the compulsory education system in Norway has been structured by this question. It explains our emphasis on the need to build up a central evaluation and information system.

Curriculum improvement and the testing issues

At the time of the 1974 review, the abolition of testing in the schools was regarded as "one of the major achievements of Norwegian policy". This aspiration can be linked with the determination to remove the divisive elements of the traditional school pattern. Since then, testing has remained an issue, particularly among those who fear that the broadening of educational objectives will lead to a reduction of standards (see below). The countervailing anxiety is that the reintroduction of testing will narrow the curriculum to that which is testable, and cause a regression to the norm in both range and the quality of education.

The reforms in the 1970s abandoned the ranking of pupil performance according to a one-dimensional, numerical scale which was felt to be a primitive form of feedback to pupils and parents. There is still testing followed by feedback to pupils which is believed to be far more meaningful to all parties than a formal system of marking. It is felt that it increases the information to people outside the school about what the school is trying to achieve. Such diagnostic and formative methods of testing might help teachers to identify students in need of special help. Standardized tests are available to teachers who want to test their own assessment of pupils.

Testing evokes two sets of issues. It can be directed primarily at the performance of the pupils; and we have already referred to the potential feedback on teaching. It can also be directed towards evaluation of institutions, local authorities or, indeed, the system as a whole. Both purposes are legitimate and we refer later to the possibility of light sampling testing which could enable the authorities at different levels to check on key sectors of achievement without harmful feedback on the individuals concerned.

Such use of testing places it in a broader context of evaluation and curriculum development. But for these ambitious goals to be realised, teachers would have to be secure in a good knowledge of their subjects and of the methods and professional ethics evoked by testing and evaluation.

In Chapter V we suggest ways in which evaluation might be advanced at the different levels of the system; testing is a key element in teacher and managerial self-knowledge.

Co-operation with parents and the community

As part of the loosening up of a centrally-controlled system, the authorities have encouraged the growth of a parental role in the schools. In particular, it was hoped that "co-operation committees" would lead to closer teacher-parent co-operation. The Ministry has asked the relevant Councils to initiate training in school development for the representatives of pupils and parents. Pilot experiments are to be started.

We were told by teachers that whilst they attempted to make the schools open to parents, meetings were often thinly attended and even stronger attempts at co-operation had failed. This is, indeed, an experience familiar to many school systems and always seems connected with issues of power. Co-operation can involve teachers consulting parents about their children and making the school open to observation; or it can mean much more. In some countries (e.g. the United Kingdom) parents on governing bodies are given a say in determining the curriculum. It may well be that as the 1987 *Mønsterplan* confers more discretion on schools, stronger moves in this direction could be attempted in Norway. If parents have no direct say over what happens in the schools, and can do no more than to observe freely and consult about their own children, it is not surprising that they read this as a message to leave all of the important issues to the professionals. Co-operation with parents is, however, only one aspect of schools' relationships with the wider society. Parents are, of course, a principal client of the schools, the work of which may well be frustrated without the co-operation of the pupils' families. It is widely recognised, however, that the school must also move within a society whose boundaries go well beyond the catchment of its own pupils and their parents. Contact with the wider community is difficult to achieve, if only because it is often difficult to define who the community is. But, taking note of the criticism that the Norwegian school is too often seen as the exclusive province of teachers, it does seem important that contact with employers, the politicians and officials who are responsible for municipal services other than education, the trades unions and other institutions within the public domain should be encouraged. The school is a key public institution whose mandate would become the stronger the more effectively it works with and admits to its processes of consultation and development the groups and the institutions of the wider social world. This is all the more important in view of the increasing heterogeneity, ethical and social, of the clients to whom the school must cater.

We noted, but were unable to pursue, the proposal that school leadership patterns should be adjusted to allow for rule by teachers' 'collectives'. This is a proposal which touches on deep questions of the accountability of professionals to democratically led systems as against the rights of teachers to develop their own values and work within them. In our judgement, however, there are as yet such uncertainties in the newly decentralised system about the relative role of head teachers, teachers, local authority administrators and politicians that such moves should be made with caution. The question of where accountability for the school is located — who will answer for its performance and to whom — is hardly perceived as an issue in Norway as yet.

Upper secondary education

The creation of a comprehensive system for upper secondary schools is a notable Norwegian achievement. Its establishment and expansion have become a key element of reform and one accepted by all political parties. In 1986 there were 163 000 applicants of whom 71 per cent (116 000) gained admittance. The numbers have increased by over 45 per cent in the last ten years. Their achievements are close to the spirit of the educational reform movement because they have also helped to substantiate educational opportunity at the local level. They are also very complex institutions coping with many conflicting objectives and pressures. There is said to be a mismatch between what students want to study and what society needs. Recruiting for teaching some of the shortage crafts is difficult. Teacher training is not well matched to the needs of the new schools. It is proving difficult to dislodge students from traditional gender roles.

Upper secondary school teachers feel that they have to face many conflicting objectives. These include education in basic subjects, cultural heritage, scientific knowledge and democratic values. They have to offer simultaneously a large number of general and vocational "lines". General education has to be integrated with more specialised education and practice in a system in which students alternate between education and work. The upper secondary schools have yet to develop services which provide information about education and effective personal counselling. We were told that many of these challenges have to be met in spite of unsatisfactory and obsolete equipment.

The context has changed radically, too. They are under challenge to meet the demands of the world of employment. It is often not easy to provide an optimum combination of options within individual pupil programmes. They are required to integrate special education with that provided for the majority of pupils. There are new immigrant groups to be absorbed and integrated into the life of the school. They are expected to adopt new teaching methods, to co-operate with parents, to move from traditional academic education towards project training. In general, the upper secondary school still has to find its way from the more traditional and selective patterns towards the creation of a meaningful comprehensive school for those above the age of 16.

Teachers feel that they have faced these challenges with insufficient resources. There are difficulties in recruiting able graduates as teachers, given the competition created by salaries in the private sector. This particularly affects the teachers of technical subjects.

While political support for the common upper secondary school is strong, the schools feel that they are subject to unconstructive criticism; moving from the selective pattern has been an enormously difficult step now largely taken.

Upper secondary education is organised in nine different areas of study in which foundation courses lead to advanced courses. Pupils choose either the general area of study or one of the vocational areas. They can also choose combinations of both. An important element of upper secondary schools is that young people in a wide range of technical and vocational areas can now choose whether they wish to remain in the upper secondary school, or receive their education at their place of work, or by a combination of both. A school might give basic education while a company can provide more specialised training and experience.

Some controversies must be noted. It is not easy for students to choose untraditional combinations of subjects. Students on vocational courses complain, as did one student leader, that they have to continue with general subjects, but the authorities believe that a broader foundation still will be desirable. Co-operation between schools and industry seems well established by general standards but complaints from employers are heard.

The Upper Secondary School Council is engaging in a continuous process of updating the schools. New models of subjects will be tried out as from 1988. There will be trials of new general subject areas. Other examples include joint work with employers in construction subjects and leadership training.

Norway has also established an ambitious programme, started in the 1980s, for the introduction of computers in schools and the updating of teachers in information technology. We came across evidence of this initiative in more than one institution. The national project involved experimental activity in selected schools, development and testing of programmes and aids, mutual co-operation between institutions and building up a national network. The OECD reviewers (1987) found some gaps between the objectives and practical pedagogical ideas and guidelines on how to reach them. They expressed cautions about generalising the results for the whole system but noted how the programme had achieved a great deal in a short period of time.

Meeting the anxiety about standards

We received conflicting evidence about the standards of schooling in Norway. Evidence of anxiety about them in some quarters was manifest. The demands for "back to the basics" had a familiar ring; it was voiced by employers, by those receiving students into higher education, and by some pupils themselves. Some maintained that pupils no longer were required to work hard enough. Although pupils evidently enjoyed good relationships with their teachers, some older students volunteered the thought that school was insufficiently demanding and did not allow them to work individually outside the teacher-led setting. "This is a place to be, and not a place to work". Teachers and teacher trainers, however, maintained that pupils were now required to undertake far more demanding work than in previous generations and that the schools faced far more complex social objectives and tasks than those previously asked of them. Taken in all, it was pointed out, the system had advanced educational opportunity. The majority of young people now enter upper secondary schools – a system just getting underway in 1974. Drop-out rates are low. Norway, in spite of all its difficulties, has greatly increased access to higher education. These changes must be an index of a growth in educability. Pupils leaving the lower and upper secondary schools are thought to have better general knowledge but to be less competent in specific skills and in the display of specialised knowledge.

In the time available to us we could not adjudicate between these different versions. We do know, however, that even good education is never good enough. The fact that there is anxiety should be enough to evoke action from the schools, from the local authorities and from the Ministry. In other parts of this report, we enumerate ways to school improvement. We briefly mention them here. First, school leadership needs to be reinforced through the better definition of the role of principals and encouraging schools to consider how more effectively to practise the greatly extended responsibilities imposed by the 1987 *Mønsterplan*. Secondly, local authorities need to benefit from the policy of decentralisation in positive and creative ways. We noted with appreciation the proposals of the Association of Local Authorities for collective efforts to develop and encourage good practice. At present local authorities sustain a role essentially concerned with control over resources and over jurisdictional matters. They need to also incorporate the functions of educational leadership, of evaluating and monitoring the progress of the schools, and of encouraging schools to be both self-critical and confident and developmental. This raises questions about the viability of local authorities for their new role, given the proliferation of authorities for the primary and lower secondary schools.

Finally, teachers, and particularly young teachers, should be well supported and counselled and not left to find their own way. In particular, teachers just leaving initial teacher training should be regarded as being at the beginning and not at the end of the acquisition of professional attitudes and skills. We were surprised to hear that there was no effective period of probation and counselling in these early years of teaching work.

Equality in the schools

Egalitarian values are strong in Norwegian society and the schools. The vast majority of Norwegians attend the locally provided public school and this is a prime objective of the system. It is heartening to note how in this widely dispersed country so many continue their education to 18 or 19. The school is seen, and has in fact acted, as the agent of equality.

Access to higher education has made notable strides. If sexual differentiation in terms of the subjects taken in school and in higher education still remains, the problems are those of individual and family conditioning as much as encouragement through policy pronouncements.

It is possible to view equality as possessing several different forms. Most systems have worked hard, but not all as successfully, as the Norwegian in securing *equality of access*. This has been called *equality of opportunity* or the "soft" or "weak" concept of equality. It is concerned with making sure that all have a chance at least to compete for desirable forms of education. In Norway the evidence for its achievement is clear; for example, it is possible for students to transfer from regional colleges to university. Many of Norway's problems result from a determination to ensure that schooling will be available as near as possible to pupils even in remote areas and this has meant, in fact, positive discrimination inasmuch as higher unit costs can be found in the areas of greater need. At the same time the emphasis on localism must mean that many students do not have access to the most important centres of adult training. *Positive discrimination* is the "hard", or the "strong" concept of equality, and seeks to deliberately reinforce the weakest in the society so that they will have a chance to make up for social and family disadvantage and thus be capable of achieving equality of outcomes. In its policies for recent immigrant groups, for indigenous minorities such as the Samis, although not seen to be sufficient in the eyes of some, and in the prolific distribution of higher education facilities, Norway has moved well towards positive or strong concepts of equality. These are, however, essentially measures of social engineering. Large-scale policies affecting the whole system have been courageously tackled with the exercise of political will and the willing expenditure of resources. Laws have been passed, resources have been donated, and structures have been changed. But we now invite the Norwegian authorities to think of a further stage of equality. This will be concerned less with the inputs of resources and changes of structure and more with the outcomes in terms of individual take-up and benefit. And at this point the methods of social engineering and of systems change cease to be the focus and questions of the quality of provision for individual pupils given by individual teachers become paramount. Thus we envisage schools putting resources into ensuring that all children are fully assessed for their needs, and their wishes and demands, so that effective tutorial care will ensure that each individual gets what he or she needs. A key example is that of integrated special education, but it applies over the whole range of schooling.

Such policies touch directly on qualitative changes in the classroom. Generalised objectives for education must then become particularised. For example, teacher training cannot secure good education in the schools if teachers are trained in a large range of subjects with the right to opt out of some of the essentials.

A system for equality could ensure that the Ministry creates the framework through which all local authorities and their schools are endowed with adequate finance, buildings, a range of teacher complexes and legitimacy and law enabling them to do their work. This may not be possible with a plethora of small authorities. At the local authority and institutional level the school needs to be a total system capable of working with parents and pupils on what they need as individuals. They can thus take up problems arising from gender or ethnic differentiation and ensure that both the social objectives and the more specific skill objectives of education are fully met.

Gender equality

Many of the strongest efforts towards equality now concern equality between the genders. For the most part the problem is the universal one of encouraging women to choose from the whole range of subject preferences in the lower and upper secondary schools and in higher education. The official policies are clear enough and institutions are in no doubt of the policy. The problems are now largely those of individual preference, to be tackled at the level of individual counselling and encouragement. There are also employer and workforce prejudices concerning, for example, apprenticeships in certain trades, problems, however, outside the competence of the education system.

Minority groups

The Sami people have their own advisory council and system. But they face the familiar problem of a small minority culture resisting the pressures of the majority. They number about 20 000 but only 1 500 are taught in Sami. Of these only 50 per cent will use it as their mother tongue. Plainly the authorities have a problem in reconciling the demands of a proud indigenous culture and the minority appeal of the education facilities, already underused, that must be provided for it. 90 000 Norwegians come from other countries, two-thirds from Europe and 22 000 from Asia and Africa. Less than 50 per cent have been offered tuition in the Norwegian language: the Ministry offered to meet the costs but municipalities did not take up the policy. Parents are not always informed of their rights. Yet much good work is being done, as we saw for ourselves in one school where a class was being conducted by two teachers, one working in the children's home tongue.

Special education

There is a considerable surge in interest in special education and the government and local authorities are determined to integrate it with the education for children not suffering from handicaps. The existence of a National Centre undertaking research as well as advanced training in special education, with 550 students and 80 staff, bears testimony to the importance accorded to these developments.

We were not able to become acquainted with special education except through our visit to the National Centre and here we rely upon the OECD appraisal made in 1983 which, however, raised points whose relevance carries over into general educational policy in Norway.

The 1983 reviewers noted the firm political commitment to change. Special education had been made part of basic education in 1975 on a decision by the Storting in 1972 that "to the extent that differentiation is needed the main approach should be individual differentiation within heterogeneous classes or in temporary groups within the class". Their separation would not be allowed. This policy was reinforced by the ending of the specific grants for special classes which drastically reduced their numbers. We were also told that a large percentage of students choose special education as a special subject in their teacher training and that more advanced courses are also available for teachers in the schools.

The political commitment is not limited to the notion of integration within education but takes for granted that it will lead to the integration of those with special needs within society as a whole. Yet the 1983 reviewers found a great variety of practices, and a reluctance to bring to an end the local special schools or institutions; indeed, some were being built as they visited. They were anxious that there should be a stronger evaluation of practice, possibly through the Primary and Lower Secondary School Council, and dissemination of findings to the schools and to the psycho-pedagogical service. They also noted that whilst parents had strong statutory rights they found it difficult to operate them. The reviewers noted some ambivalence among some teachers and parents about integration on the grounds that special schools would secure more resources for pupils with particular needs than could the general schools. They also found in 1983 that specific criteria for the choice of children to be integrated were not clear.

In this area, it is, indeed, difficult to reconcile practicalities with good social policy. The development of special education everywhere was, in its time, a triumph of diagnosis of social and personal problems and the allocation of special and usually generous resources indicated a desire to help disadvantaged members of society. In moving away from specialist provision towards integration, problems of definition, of pedagogical practice, of parental involvement and of allowing for special help through the individualisation of general practice are all major challenges for any system.

IV

POLICY CHANGES AND OBJECTIVES IN HIGHER AND ADULT EDUCATION

Expansion of higher education. Access

In a period of ten years, Norway's total student body in higher education has increased by about 45 per cent. In 1984 there were 93 500 students of whom nearly 17 000 worked part-time. The student body divides between 42 000 places in the universities and 51 500 in the college sector. A 1984 White Paper aimed for a student body of 100 000 by 1995, but in 1986 the figures were increased to 105 000. It is also hoped to recruit more foreign students and to maintain significant numbers of Norwegian students abroad.

There is much to admire in these developments and plans. For one thing, the whole increase in the student body over the last decade is the result of recruiting more women. Their share of places in 1984 was nearly 50 per cent compared with 24 per cent in 1973. Whilst, as do other countries, the Norwegian authorities regret and look for ways of changing the gender balance in technology and economics, in medicine and natural science more equal representation is developing rapidly. Differentiation between boys and girls in the lower and upper secondary school has long been gone. Many of the surviving problems of gender differentiation seem associated with issues outside the remit of the education services: patterns of family obligation, and traditional role allocations can only in part be met by policies of encouragement and education towards the exercise of greater choice.

Norway stands well, but in no sense in the lead of its European counterparts, in the expansion of access to higher education. Norway's recruitment rates are not high when compared with countries of similar size, social composition and political make-up. The direct recruitment from secondary school was 22 per cent in 1984. It had reached 26 per cent in 1974 and dropped to 16 per cent in 1981. Entry is competitive to many courses in both regional colleges and universities. The authorities note a flagging demand for some courses which is worrying and which leads us to consider critically some of the special features of Norwegian higher education development.

In part, flagging demand can be attributed to Norwegian economic success. Competent young people are able to find remunerative employment without the benefit of a full undergraduate education. They may take shorter courses, or no courses at all, and find their way into a good income. Whether that position will survive the likely change in the economic climate we can only guess. Students also find it increasingly difficult to live on the funds available to them, although expenditure on aid has increased greatly in recent years, and seem reluctant to finance their higher education by loan. The solution of this problem would have led us to a detailed analysis involving potentially contentious political judgements. It seems unlikely that the existing system is, however, working well. Other and more deep-seated problems would probably bear closer examination. The patterns of relationships between higher education teachers and their students, the quality of teaching accommodation, the extent to which the curriculum is well updated are all factors likely to bear upon the difficulties that institutions have in retaining students.

The phenomenon of reduced demands raises questions about the esteem in which higher education is held in Norway. In other countries, such as the United States, the United Kingdom, France, Sweden and Japan, some of whose employment and economy are relatively buoyant, employers and young people seeking employment alike regard the achievement of a high level of post-school education as the key to better, more prestigious and more useful employment. The fact that this is not so in Norway links to more general perceptions of higher education. We must emphasize that we did not, and could not, assess the quality of higher education in Norway. What we have to say here depends upon what we were told by those we met, both central politicians and administrators and academics in the institutions. We sensed, therefore, because we would not fully analyse, what was implied in the report of the Norwegian authorities, namely, that higher education had somehow not achieved, or has slipped from, its rightful place in Norwegian society. We were also told in some of our discussions what two students of the Norwegian higher education system have written: "Many politicians seem to have regarded the universities as cumbersome; slowly adapting establishments, generally lacking the ability to adjust to new social needs: educational innovation has had to take place elsewhere, with the result that they were accorded low priority as compared to most institutions. The strong focus on decentralisation has pushed the university somewhat into the background, and surprisingly enough, they were largely unable to defend their interests."[1] After a period of political favour and expansion the universities are thought to have become dispirited and to have found it difficult to take the initiative.

The four universities represent a very wide range of style, of scholarly reputation and achievement, and of application towards social and economic objectives. Collectively, however, quite unlike those in other countries, where universities or equivalent high-level centres of research, scholarship and teaching are reckoned to be the gateway to leadership roles in society, the Norwegian universities seem to be at something of a discount. Many of the functions which one would expect to see being carried out by the oldest and largest, the University of Oslo, with 20 000 students, are to be found in independently financed and run Institutes for Research. Major new areas of development and teaching, such as in management and business studies, are promoted by private institutions whose success has been phenomenal and, as far as we can judge from the independent evaluation made of one of them, well earned.

To some extent, this recession from self-confidence and a leadership role can be laid at the doors of the academics themselves. But at one university we visited it seemed possible for academics to aim for the dual goals of high standards of academic excellence and of meeting the needs of society and of the economy.

Higher education, and particularly the universities, seems to need to refresh its social mandate. By this we mean that some kind of social contract between them and the State, representing the society that both ought to serve, should be made. This should state more emphatically the holistic nature of university work. The universities must have the capacity to research, to codify critically existing scholarship, to teach to the highest possible levels so that they will replenish themselves with the ambitions and work of the able young. Any university teacher who does not feel confident that he or she is recruiting students better than himself is in a sense failing. The universities need free monies, the ability to give time to those who will advance and criticise and revolutionise systems of work and thought in society, in the world of science and in the economy. But in return for that mandate of freedom, backed by Kroners, the university must be willing to take on programmes of research that do not eschew the practical and the useful, that do not rest on artificial dichotomies between the theoretical and the applied, and which do not confuse the esoteric with the elegant. They must be open to allow for the wider access which Norwegian society needs and demands for women, newly arrived ethnic minorities and older students from generations insufficiently educated; good starts have already been made on that latter element of the social compact.

In return for this, the Norwegian public authorities would be entitled to realise the enormous capacities within the universities which should be, if not always the first port of call for research efforts, at least a principal source of advice and scientific development. Whether their financing should be predominantly undertaken through the research councils or through sectoral grants of monies in return for specific work, or through free monies embodied in the core finance of the universities, we are not competent to judge within the Norwegian framework. But multiple sources reducing dependence on a single Ministry should be fostered and academics encouraged to secure funds from them.

Whilst the expansion of higher education has been formidable it is recognised that reform has been piecemeal and in need of review. Policy has strongly favoured regional development, yet the eastern area, and particularly the region of Oslo, has grown most, so that 70 per cent of the population live there. This has resulted in the University of Oslo being too overloaded to fulfill all of the functions to be expected of the largest and oldest of the universities in the present era of change. The pressure of teaching large numbers is said to contribute to a relative reduction in research effort. Increased capacity for applied research and development in the regional colleges and the development of non-university research institutes has weakened the research profiles of the universities although, of course, there are many examples of distinguished individuals and departments.

In various ways the universities do not feel that they are masters of their own destinies. The universities feel that they are restricted by state controls, which are said to be handled lightly and which the most vigorous may circumvent but which, to outsiders, seem incompatible with the notion of free institutions able to both support and act as responsible critics of existing scientific and social states. It is, for example, bizarre that institutions are not free, once global budgets are determined, to specify their own establishments. All teaching posts must be approved by Parliament and professors are appointed by the King. No doubt the collegium rules on most important matters and, indeed, just at the time that other systems are moving towards a sometimes unreflecting managerialism, the power of Senates remains strong; Rectors are elected by the collegium or faculty boards. But that is again a Norwegian style paradox: the State still broods over the universities exercising controls whilst within the internal structures prodigious feats of academic leadership – and we have heard of such – may be required to move the institution and its components to change.

It is, however, possible for the universities to experience the changes which are occurring in other countries. The second largest university, Bergen, is entrepreneurial and looks to both its region and to multinational bodies for their sponsorship of development. At the same time it is making strong efforts to encourage interdisciplinary work and has committees searching for integrative academic themes. Some 10 per cent of its budget comes from commissioned research. The other universities, too, are extending the span of their commissioned research and other socially-related work. Bergen was almost wholly concerned with producing secondary school teachers when first founded in 1945. It is now expanding its doctoral programmes, the numbers of students in which are certainly small in Norwegian universities. It still feels constrained in the quality of its library and in the time available to faculty for research. But it is making strong efforts to develop itself both academically and as part of the system for economic development.

Higher education must now contend with the smaller age groups which will be reaching it in the 1990s, a reduction in demand accentuated by the fact that, in distinction from many countries, its young people do not favour study within the longer courses, but instead go to courses in the areas demanding lower skills.

Structure

Apart from the universities there are specialised institutions with university status. There are then the regional colleges offering courses of two or three years' duration. They are organised under a system of regional college boards, one for each county. They contain representatives of the county, of college employees and students who are all appointed by the Ministry, of employers and unions, as well as the main institutional interests, including the universities. Courses are allocated to meet local demands, but the data about the demands and the financial allocations are not strong. The Ministry retains controls over student numbers and buildings. Appointments of staff are made by the boards. Under the regional board there are also a large number of teacher training colleges, colleges of technology and specialist colleges for nursing, social work, catering and the like.

The total number of higher education institutions was 228 in 1984, including the universities and specialised institutions. The large majority of institutions are very small. Only 10 institutions, including the universities, have more than 1 000 students and they enrol half the student body. Both Conservative and Labour governments have advanced the case for consolidating institutions but regional opposition is expressed through groups in Parliament, irrespective of political colour. More recently, a commission under Professor Hernes has been established and the issue of consolidation is among its terms of reference.

If the universities are said to be uncertain of their role and even depressed about it, the Norwegian people can congratulate itself on the astonishing development of the regional colleges.

One complaint which we have heard is that resources and political support have been so devoted to the regional colleges and other institutions associated with the regional boards that the universities have suffered. Certainly the regional and other local colleges which we visited are full of confidence. They speak of their research programmes and some expect to create doctoral programmes (at a time when Norwegian higher education at large is only just embarking upon an expansion of the doctorate as training for research workers). One we visited was involved in training and development for the fishing industry and also had a well recruited Master's course in business administration. It was vigorously building up a programme of applied research and saw itself as being much the same as an American state university. But it did not think of itself as "just a consulting shop". It wanted the resources for its teaching to be linked to its research efforts. Apart from its regional affiliations, it was building up connections with Finnish, Swedish, Icelandic and Canadian institutions.

As far as research efforts are concerned, we feel that they would be better described as research and development than as research in its generally accepted sense. Thus, we noted with interest one college of education which was helping teachers develop project work in the schools in response to the provisions of the 1987 *Mønsterplan*. The College of Engineering at Bergen provides advice to and secures student placements in a salmon farm which depends upon a range of disciplines for its technical development. These are admirable developments; research policy is best considered as many-layered and admitting a wide range of theory and practice. Good local research and development work can depend upon fundamental science and test it. The use of higher education as a contribution towards the economic, social and political life of the regions is a wholly appropriate exploitation of a human resource for which Norwegians pay good money. Our concern is, therefore, not with the development of the regional colleges but with the corollaries of their development.

The connections between the universities and the regional colleges should be confirmed and strengthened. The universities serve as training grounds for researchers who can then take their place in the teaching and research and development functions of the more local institutions. There might be a tendency for the central authorities to believe that because they have encouraged research in the regions, as well as in the independently funded institutions, the universities can be left to go their own way.

Whilst there is some disassociation between the universities and the regional colleges, we should notice encouraging features of the Norwegian system. Thus, students from the regional or other more local colleges can transfer with relative freedom to university undergraduate courses. Whilst in virtually every other country there is a hierarchy of esteem between institutions, students in those areas where there are no universities nearby (and that means a larger part of the land mass of Norway) do not aspire to find their way to Oslo or Bergen or Trondheim or Tromsø if there is an adequate regional course nearby. Thus a parity of esteem among students, their parents and employers has been achieved.

This seems to be a wholly admirable development but we place two reservations against it. First, the ablest students will not, in the nature of regional college development, have access to the ablest academics or to the best libraries or laboratories in the formative periods of their lives. The recruitment of an academic elite, which can be divorced from the un-Norwegian notion of a social elite, does seem to require early encounter, of the ablest young mathematicians or philosophers or physicists with the ablest scholars in their field. Secondly, we earlier quoted Dr. Ingrid Eide as implying that Norwegians did not believe in too much geographical or social mobility. But the fact is that young people are more on the move than in previous eras. If the able young or any others seeking higher education are locked into local provision which offers only a limited range of subjects, geographical immobility will be compounded by intellectual restriction.

For these reasons, we believe that there should be far more positive attempts to integrate the university and the regional systems. Some stratification and differentiation of function seem necessary, and once that is done appropriate and vigorous links between both the work and the people doing it could then be considered.

Within the areas of technical specialisation, the hierarchy is more clear. Thus a regional college of engineering will see itself as more clearly at a lower level than a national specialist college producing fully qualified professional engineers. Such institutions perform valuable functions in both producing skilled manpower and in applied R&D in such areas as the engineering components of salmon farming. They do not feel themselves too strongly constrained by the Ministry but would like more sabbatical time and resources for applied work. They also have anxieties about the level of preparation of some of the students reaching them.

The social role of higher education varies greatly according to the fields of study and the institution. Its critics believe that it could achieve much more with changes in organisation and motivation. Some believe that departments should begin to examine and state their objectives. Some of the detailed reforms that are underway which need speeding up include building up of graduate studies so that the system can recruit well qualified teachers and researchers. It seems difficult, for example, to reconcile the ambitions of regional colleges to engage in research and to offer graduate and even doctoral programmes with the weakness of the post-graduate training system.

Yet a further problem is that students are opting for the shorter courses which will lead to immediate employment. It is good that the institutions can meet a range of demand with such flexibility but quite a serious problem that the ablest young people do not feel it worthwhile to graduate at a level from which they might be able to fill the national needs for highly-qualified senior professionals and academics.

Many of these issues are to be considered by the Hernes Commission on higher education which is likely to produce its recommendations before this report is published. Change in the structural aspects of Norwegian higher education will require the exercise of strong political will in view of the local community aspirations embodied in present arrangements.

Single-subject institutions

A further reflection of the decentralised and differentiated nature of Norwegian higher education is the persistence of a large number of single-subject institutions. This contrasts with the practice of those countries which have integrated the teaching of such subjects as the training of social workers or of teachers into broader based multi-purpose institutions. The arguments are not solely economic, although savings from scale are not to be ignored; students are able to participate in broader-based courses in the first or second year of their undergraduate life and thus have access to more generous educational and social experiences. They can also exercise choice somewhat later in their undergraduate career before deciding which vocational line to follow. Teaching in general arts and science subjects for those ultimately specialising in vocational courses can be given by specialists in the subjects. We noted the continued proliferation of separate and often quite small schools offering courses leading to particular vocations and professions, even when new general regional or other colleges were being built alongside. This seemed to us to be potentially wasteful and limiting although we were not able, of course, to go into the particular social and political reasons for these decisions. We note that policy is moving towards consolidation but, from the Background Report, that there is also some reluctance in endorsing this principle. This is especially the case for teacher training colleges.

Central policy-making

We encountered some criticism of central policy-making for higher education. Certainly, central authorities themselves consider that there is a need for wholesale review and the Hernes Commission is expected to provide that. We can most easily give our perspective of what is needed by specifying some of the things that we think the centre should do; this does not imply that none of them is now being done.

First, the national authorities have made clear statements on access policies. They see the need to sustain and to expand recruitment to higher education of students leaving the upper secondary schools and of adults who failed to take opportunities earlier in their careers. Yet policies have worked well in terms of redressing the balance between the genders.

We feel, however, that they have not clarified fully their attitude on student recruitment and mobility in two respects. Student recruitment is flagging in part because of the pull of high employment and partly because of poor student finance. We also believe that the labour market could contribute far more towards increasing recruitment to higher education. It may be an indication of the lack of status accorded to higher education as a whole that employers do not offer differentials between those who have stuck it out for a full higher education course and those who take shorter and more instrumental sequences. Higher education does not, therefore, act as a particularly efficient screening device as is the case in many other countries. Nor is there any employer sponsorship whereby students reading courses in the shortage subjects may be sponsored by employers in return for a commitment to enter employment for at least a reasonable period after graduation. All of these issues of access are national matters to which the central authorities should give continuous attention.

Another issue of access concerns mobility. The development of regional colleges is admirable in itself. But we have already remarked that higher education, even in the most egalitarian societies, is a system which cannot avoid differentiation according to levels of both learner and teacher ability and access is needed to the facilities that major centres of higher education can give even to undergraduate students.

For the centre, however, to take grip of the relationship between university and regional college education and research, it must have a clearer view of the flows of students to those institutions, and by regions. This brings us to a further point.

The centre is moving from the administration of tight rules towards a more information-led role. It already has at its disposal the well accredited work of the Institute for Studies in Research and Higher Education in Oslo. We feel that its data base for higher education administration and development could be further extended, made more public and more explicitly related to future policy developments. This would incorporate not only studies of student flows but analyses of flows into research and into higher education teaching, with evaluations of strengths and shortfalls. It would also incorporate a research programme on organisational and institutional issues on such questions as the development of managerial patterns of leadership in relationship to the power of Senates and other collegial forms, the growth of entrepreneurial activity over the range of institutions, institutional connections between universities, regional and other non-university bodies, and relationships between the private and public sector of higher education.

We believe that the Royal Ministry of Cultural and Scientific Affairs should make a determined analysis of the web of regulations and controls with which it governs the system. Central government must govern. That is its duty and its public mandate. But in governing higher education it faces knotty problems concerning the nature of political obligations and consent. In principle, higher education institutions should contribute towards the public good by the exercise of their freedom. Shorn of its rhetoric, there has to be a negotiation between what society needs, as expressed through central government determinations, and the statement of needs and wants by regions, the employment system and the like, and what the academy can best produce within the maximum freedom. This would imply a cutting away of every shred of detailed regulation. Global budgets can be negotiated on understandings that contain generously phrased terms of reference. Institutions which do not meet the social requirement can be punished retrospectively by the withdrawal of part of their funds. But for the most part, mature institutions at the centre will benefit from the presumption that they are dealing with mature institutions at the university and college levels.

Finally, the centre has a responsibility for doing something about the political psychology of Norwegian higher education. Its universities are sadly and to some extent undeservedly lacking in public esteem and in the esteem of government. They are vital to the further development of the economy and in the education of the next generation of leaders for the society and the economy. They should be given nothing for nothing but should be encouraged to express their views on how they can best contribute towards the next wave of Norwegian social and educational development.

The system for R&D

The Norwegian system for R&D has recently been subject to a separate OECD review, and we restrict our comments here to those aspects which directly concern the education system. The five research councils work under the policies of the Royal Ministry of Cultural and Scientific Affairs. In the case of the Council for Science and the Humanities two-thirds of the budget come from the Ministry and another third from the Ministry of Environment. There is a separate Council for Applied Social Science. A half of the money goes to the universities; 4 per cent to the regional colleges; 17 per cent to other research institutions and 25 per cent indirectly to universities by way of programme grants. These finance some of the temporary university posts. The allocations are made on quality judgements and are not predetermined. The present research council policy is to shift funding from well-funded projects to well-funded milieus in which good research traditions can be built up and visiting foreign scholars attracted.

The system is felt to be short of resources, particularly for the purchase of heavy equipment, and is likely to become short of qualified manpower. In the 1970s and 1980s there was a build-up of applied science and a corresponding decrease in the budget for research. The universities were not thought to demonstrate convincingly that they could adapt to the increased demands for applied research. But the trend is now towards the government realising the need for basic research, and some universities at least are moving with the new policy steers.

It can be seen from the figures above that whilst the regional colleges may have received good treatment in respect of their teaching functions, they have no particular premium when it comes to receiving research council funds.

The OECD science review was not sparing in its criticisms of the way in which R&D related to university research. It stated that the research community needed increased coordination and steering, that it lacked long-term decisions on resources so that neither universities nor research councils could take long-term decisions. The reviewers thought that the existence of many small university departments and institutes "must be a suboptimisation". From our point of view, concerned as we are with the well-being of the teaching functions of universities, we share the view of the reviewers that some institutes might well merge with university departments. Teaching will then be better informed by current research and researchers might form part of the stock of active teachers. We also share the reviewers' belief that R&D in regional colleges can be a useful and indeed essential link between academic work and economic development. We can see no reason, however, in view of the smallness of the sums involved, why their growth should not continue whilst at the same time the research capacities of the universities are better built up.

Connections with the labour market and economy

Higher education has to meet several objectives at once. It occupies a key position in meeting the economy's needs for highly-qualified personnel. It must provide people with the knowledge and other qualities for successful participation in the life of their communities as well as for self-development. It must provide communities with the means of securing educational opportunities.

Despite the expansion which has taken place in the number of institutions, range of courses, and student enrolment, there are indications of imbalances in recent years between the demand for and availability of qualified personnel. Such imbalances are inevitable. A feature of all present-day economies is the continual shifts taking place in the structure of employment, associated with changing products and technologies. What are relevant for the education system are the speed and effectiveness with which it adapts to this changing employment environment.

Our impressions are that there is scope for improving the performance of the higher education sector in this respect. These impressions stem from some of the observations made to us as well as our own understanding of the way in which the system has been functioning. On several occasions our attention was drawn to the tendency of many students to opt for the shorter courses of study and then to seek what were perceived to be higher paid employment opportunities in the private sector. In the case of teaching the point was also made that many of the younger members of the profession have been leaving to take up private sector employment.

This example raises the issue of the appropriate intervention and response to the changing education and employment environment. It could be held that it is the students who are adapting more speedily and appropriately to these changes, since the willingness of employers to offer higher salaries for their services must reflect their value to those who would employ them. The counterview is that the attractions of short course and earlier employment will be short-lived and that the longer-run well-being of the economy calls for retaining and increasing numbers in such areas as teaching or engineering.

Although this latter view appears to be widely held among those involved in higher education there was little evidence of actions or policies to promote this outcome. In the case of teachers, for example, there are various proposals or suggestions for lengthening the period of study for initial qualification from three to four years, and for the development of various post-graduate programmes.

Whatever the general educational merits of such developments, their initial effect would be to reduce, not increase, the supply of teachers available to teach. The longer study period postpones the point at which teaching commences, while the extra costs incurred by lengthier study periods would tend to reduce the numbers enrolling for such programmes. At the same time there appeared to be little support for specific measures to encourage increased student enrolment by more generous grants, or other discriminatory financial measures.

When regarding other features of the Norwegian system the case for more flexible responses is strengthened. The emphasis on the regional facilities means that there are more staff for a given student population than would be the case in most education systems.

The rapid pace at which new knowledge is produced and demographic change occurs suggests that the more appropriate response would be perhaps to retain the length of the initial teacher education programme but to reshape the internal structure of the curriculum within its present length and introduce a strong induction period for teachers which should be followed by a compulsory sequence of in-service training. Such an approach would be more attuned to the shifting pattern of employer needs and student choices, and thus provide improved prospects of achieving better matching of demands and availabilities of qualified personnel.

There are indeed examples of developments along these lines within the higher education system, but these tend to be the exception rather than the rule, and the presence of a significant private sector in which students are faced with higher costs tends to strengthen this conclusion.

Private higher education

A further area in which a reassessment of activities and relationships might lead to more effective results is that of the role of private education. We noted the increased provision of business education by the Institute of Management. The fact that so many students are willing to accept the higher costs involved (including from 1988 the cost of supplying their own personal computer) indicates a ready demand for such courses. The manner in which the Institute expanded the courses throughout the country also suggests a high degree of flexibility in meeting actual demands as they arise. If the public sector were to respond belatedly by offering similar courses this would add to the budgetary burden of education without any obvious gain in educational performance. If, on the other hand, publicly-provided courses were to charge similar fees and other costs to those of the private institutions, this would seem to breech the notion of having courses of study open without any discriminatory financial element and would place business education at a disadvantage by comparison with other fields of study. One possible way forward would be for state support to provide student places up to some agreed limits at private institutions so that students could choose freely between different fields of study and different types of institution.

Teacher training

We have already referred to the web of circumstances within which the status of teachers is being determined. Both they and those who observe them such as employers believe that they suffer from lack of status and – we cannot take sides – salaries and conditions of service are said to contribute further towards the status problem. One possibility of enhancing status might be to integrate teacher training within large multi-purpose higher education institutions as we have suggested earlier. Indeed, the one area which is susceptible to state action is radical reappraisal of the teacher training system. We know that a Royal Commission is at present sitting on this subject.

In any event, changing social and economic conditions and the much larger expectations placed on the schools by decentralisation and the 1987 *Mønsterplan* make teacher training a key element in the preparation for change.

We were made aware of dissatisfaction with present arrangements. Students are required to take small amounts of study in the range of ten subjects which are obligatory in the schools. They spend one academic year on pedagogical theory and practice in professional training. Yet whilst many teachers must work in schools where only one or two teachers must provide the full range of basic subjects, it is not compulsory for them to take, for example, Norwegian or mathematics to any advanced level. Fifty per cent of teachers have not reached university level in the subjects they are to teach.

Two other criticisms to be made of present arrangements are, as already noted, that teacher education is often offered in single-purpose and quite small teacher training colleges and both subject specialisation and social integration with other professional entrants are therefore more difficult to achieve. Nor are young teachers supervised during a period of probation when either the local authorities or the teacher training institutions might be expected to offer a period of supervised probation.

We know that some teacher training colleges are becoming increasingly involved in school development. It does seem necessary, however, that there should be a full scale drive on in-service training which will encompass problems of school leadership, strengthening teaching in basic subjects as well as in such new subjects as information technology.

So far, there are few studies of teacher education in Norway to which we can refer but one problem noted in our examination derives from the "openness" of teacher preparation. Candidates for the profession can choose an individual study path within education courses which may mean that the schools do not get people who are qualified adequately in the areas of greatest teaching need. Nor is it clear that the more decentralised system will ensure a good link between the initial training and the in-service training of teachers.

Adult education

In the course of our short visit, we were able to enjoy only the briefest glimpse of provision for adult education. Norway is committed to sustain and expand the service although it has just gone through a period in which public funding has been allowed to decline. It is provided both by public authorities but mostly by publicly-funded voluntary organisations. While many courses are oriented towards strengthening community interests and involvement, or are geared towards leisure interests, there is also a substantial component which is relevant to formal education, in that they can provide the basis for the acquisition of various skills and qualifications. Adults may now offer single subjects for public examination, and preparation for them is the function of the voluntary organisations. They also engage in study work "unrestricted by examinations and curricula". Adult education includes Distance Education.

Adult education, and the study circles and other activities which it provides, have always been an important element of Norwegian life, particularly in communities where traditional educational facilities are not easy to sustain. The diversification of functions in the upper secondary school, which is able to recruit adult pupils, and the demographic downturn which will eventually reach higher education should not reduce the need for adult education in a society where the mass of the population received an abbreviated compulsory education.

The relationship between adult education and the extensive system of higher education is obviously an issue which needs to be further considered; there appears to be some lack of clarity about allocation of responsibilities, as well as some restrictions on the access which voluntary bodies have to the facilities of educational establishments. Since the voluntary bodies have an extensive and flexible network of activities, they might offer a convenient vehicle for meeting changing course needs in a local context. Their ability to do this would be enhanced by the development of closer working links between them and the various educational institutions. It may well be that local authorities should be more strongly encouraged to work more closely with the voluntary bodies. Adult education, particularly since it reaches so many people who might otherwise not have continuing access to education, could be used to meet not only the cultural needs of individuals but the needs of the economy for more trained manpower. For this to happen, the links with regional and local colleges would have to become stronger. It is already possible to transfer credits earned through the adult education system to regular programmes at the regional colleges if the voluntary body and college agree the arrangements.

The role of the intellectual in Norway

Our thinking about higher and adult education reflects more general concerns about the role of the intellectual in society. Norwegians have always respected learning and scholarship and the contributions of artists to literature and the arts. The strong adherence to democratic forms of working, in which social class is at a relative discount and the opinions of all citizens are respected, is also part of a tradition which reflects itself in the workings of the education system. Hence the diffusion of power to many local authorities and a reluctance to consolidate institutions artificially.

At the same time, in the making of the Norwegian State consensus was incorporated into a web of centralised regulation and produced a uniform curriculum for the schools. Movements towards freer forms of working, represented in the 1987 *Mønsterplan* and in the development of co-operation with parents, are likely to be a long and arduous process of undoing the tradition of a centrally formed consensus.

Higher education does not easily incorporate consensus. At its best, it challenges received notions, is defiant of accepted truths, is eager to falsify received theory and replace it by knowledge and theory which is ever on the move. Its place in a free society is to offer critique, in the positive sense of that word, of both science and society. In so doing, it must constantly look to its own legitimacy and its mandate must constantly be negotiated with the State which finds funds and security for it. But a good society cherishes and succours its own critics and therefore sponsors the role of the freestanding intellectual.

We have the impression that Norwegian intellectuals in general and within higher education in particular, in no sense suffer a lack of freedom. But the feeling of constraint imposed by state regulation, and the disassociation of free research from teaching makes them less capable of contributing to society from the strongest vantage point that higher education should offer.

It is thus for the central authorities and higher education, and particularly the universities, to consider the renewed mandate to which we referred earlier.

NOTE

1. S. Kyvik and H. Skoie (1982), "Recent Trends in Norwegian Education", *European Journal of Education*, Vol. 17, No. 2.

V

STRUCTURE AND GOVERNANCE

Decentralisation: The conflict between localism and policy planning

The Norwegian authorities have made enormous strides towards releasing local authorities and the schools from detailed central control. In Chapters II and III we referred to the new objectives set for schools and the ways in which the 1987 *Mønsterplan* would confer on them both the benefits and the rigours of freedom to develop local variations of a national curriculum. At the same time, the regions or counties and municipalities or communities have been given freedom to run their schools without the national controls exercised by regional directors. They will soon negotiate salaries with teachers as employers, acting through their association, and the development of education in their areas is largely in their own hands. They form part of the multi-purpose local authorities receiving a general grant from the centre which they must allocate between different purposes including those concerned with education. These are massive changes intended to make local politicians, administrators and teachers fully responsible for their own political and professional affairs.

The potential difficulties resulting from such changes need to be noted. The centre has used its power to allocate to ensure that equality has been a reality in the vast land mass of Norway. But now that it is for local authorities to decide, the poorer areas, no matter how well funded, will have to face the consequences of maintaining small schools providing education for a few children. Because there is no effective system for monitoring standards it cannot know whether the standards of education in the different areas will be commensurate with each other.

Until recently the central authorities and Parliament were able to assert the needs of education within each area. The adoption of a general grants system in 1986 will mean that education must compete with other services, and particularly to an increasingly voracious health service. Moreover, whilst local politics have always been strong, the power of local politicians will become correspondingly stronger as those at the centre become weaker.

Decentralisation ought to lead to a stronger professionalisation of education and that would be a good thing in itself. At the same time, however, it seems necessary for the centre to reappraise its role, not in order to try to take back the powers that it has ceded, but to establish its influence by asserting the national norms which should be expected of all local authorities and their schools, by creating means of monitoring and evaluating and by publishing their evaluations. In this way the national planning system will strengthen its normative influence and its power to create change through information, at the same time as it reduces its prescriptions over the work of the schools.

The distribution of functions

The willingness to distribute power is manifest throughout the Norwegian education system. At the national level, responsibility is divided. The kindergartens are the responsibility of the Ministry of Consumer Affairs and Administration. The primary, lower and upper secondary schools are the province of the Ministry of Church and Education. Higher education belongs to the Ministry of Cultural and Scientific Affairs. We heard one or two comments to the effect that, as a result, educational policy is not well co-ordinated although we were also told that in so small a political community as that of Norway co-ordination across ministerial lines was not difficult to achieve. In spite of the continuing power of the centre there are complaints about the fragmentation. "New secretariats are being established all the time". There was said to be poor manpower planning so that there were serious disparities between the teachers available for different subjects.

A more serious point is, perhaps, that although the great majority of local authorities are very small, there are two tiers, the regions and the municipalities, in which the regions are responsible for upper secondary education and certain aspects of higher education whilst the municipalities are responsible for lower secondary and primary education.

Given the geographical distances it would be difficult to create local authorities large enough to acquire professional expertise and leadership and, at the same time, capable of being near to the people they serve. But we feel that it makes little sense to divide the functions in this way. We have remarked earlier that continuity of education seems to require continuity of educational leadership within local authorities. This would imply that there should be one authority for both. Moreover, if decentralisation to the schools themselves is made a reality it is difficult to see why the regional level could not relate directly to individual schools without the intervention of municipalities. The suggestion is not made simply on grounds of economy although they cannot be ignored. It is also a question of ensuring that schools are not isolated in small pockets in which professional networks, competent in-service training and access to other specialist resources are not available.

The institution

Adjusting the superstructure of central and local authorities is less important than ensuring that the school is a viable institution. If schools become fully viable and able to work out their own curriculum patterns within the broad framework of the *Mønsterplan*, and if their head teachers can offer full educational leadership, the school itself will be the most important level of the education system. If, in addition to getting its internal organisation in order so that it can fulfill a truly professional role on behalf of its clients, it creates strong relationships with parents and other clients, it will become all the stronger because more fully legitimated. Given those degrees of strength, it will be possible for local authorities, enlarged and strengthened as we have suggested, to adopt a true leadership, advisory and strategic role and to leave the main tasks of developing education to the schools themselves, subject always, however, to monitoring and evaluation by the elected component in the system.

The Norwegian authorities are expecting schools to participate in a deliberate programme of innovation and development. The newly-established Co-ordination Committee for School Development has in its data base a total of 3 000 projects. But, as the Background Report remarks, there seems to be a gap between the developing schools and the schools which have so far not moved. We also agree with the national authorities that in this area there is need to continually consider the balance between locally-governed school development and that which is encouraged by the centre. At the same time, through the Molis Project, leadership development in the school community is being encouraged through a six-year programme.

Co-operation and leadership

Earlier in this report we noted the Norwegian authorities' regret that schemes of co-operating, intended to bring parents more closely into the life of the schools, had been unsuccessful. If schools become stronger because of self-evaluation and because they command the right to develop key points of their own curriculum, they will also become sufficiently confident to work with the other concerned groups in determining the curricular and social life of the school. It would be advantageous if Norway could join those other OECD countries which are taking steps in this direction.

The role of the centre: policy-making and management

The Norwegian authorities have put a great deal of political effort and potential resources into decentralising. In their terms, they are attempting to move from governing through rules to governing through the setting of goals.

At its best, decentralisation should mean the building up of strong institutions which are responsive to the social good, as defined through the national consensus, which work purposefully towards helping clients define their needs and meeting them, and through the professional and expert development and delivery of the curriculum. If decentralisation goes well, each school can then become a centre of policy and practice capable of determining its own style and forms of expertise and contributing its own value positions to those of the larger society.

The Norwegian government has moved with great determination towards these ends but in so doing has left behind many issues that need urgent but sensitive treatment. In the first place, decentralisation has left central government with an uncertain role at a time when it should be developing a new but challenging place for itself in the policy system. Secondly, decentralisation has not been specified sufficiently for the school and the local authority to take on their new and difficult tasks.

Within a decentralised scheme what might be the role of the centre? Plainly it must retain control over the distribution of resources. Norway has chosen the route of general grants and has thus moved away from detailed control over the specific award of monies for particular purposes. This is the right procedure in principle although it will be noted that other countries which have adopted a system of general grants find that sooner or later some areas must then be returned to specificity if national objectives are to be met. But the granting of general rather than earmarked or specific monies does not emancipate the centre from the responsibility for stating its views on what policies those monies should be used to promote. Thus a general grant award to local authorities must contain certain "hypothecations" about changes in policy affecting the whole of Norway; there is good reason for such hypothecations to be declared so that local authorities will not be in doubt about how the money has been made up and what policies the central government hopes the local authorities will achieve.

Moreover, the centre still has a key role in the determination of school curricula. The *Mønsterplan* is created through a consensual process in which schemes are submitted for widespread consultation and the responses are taken into account. The government and Parliament eventually determine it, but the role of the Ministry in its formulation cannot be denied. Also, the Ministry proposes the law, still so important in Norwegian educational policy-making and practice, and ensures that it is administered.

All of these functions, and many more, remain within the Ministry, but the examiners perceived what can be described as a lack of a clear ideological role for the Ministry. Very general objectives are easy to state. General statements of objectives, however, without a carefully prepared background of knowledge of what is happening in the schools, of policy analysis for the present and for the future, will remain vacuous and leave the centre as hostage to the interests with whom they, rightly and conscientiously, negotiate.

It may well be that expertise is provided through the connections between the Ministry and its Advisory Councils. That will depend, however, upon their composition and the balance which they offer between expertise and the representation of interests contained within them. They might represent opinions difficult to reconcile with the analytic approaches of central planning. Both are necessary, but need to be held in good balance. But we felt that more definite analytic positions could have been taken by the central planners so that they could moderate and interact more powerfully with those whom they consulted.

In general, we felt that it must be difficult for the Ministry to be fully accountable for the analysis and promotion of educational values and for ensuring standards in education. Indeed it must be impossible to ensure that standards are achieved if there is no direct knowledge at the centre of what in fact the schools are doing. This in no sense is an argument for prescription by the centre. The power of the centre in a decentralised system should be normative rather than prescriptive and this would mean that they are able to join in and lead the debate on objectives because they are in the best position to know what is happening throughout Norway.

Monitoring and evaluation

This leads us, therefore, to think about the ways in which the Ministry can secure better knowledge of the working of the system. First, it needs a far more secure quantitative data base enabling it to know how the resources it distributes are used. It needs, too, to have more secure knowledge about the part played by educational institutions in the flow of students and of their access to institutions of different levels. We heard, for example, that the regional colleges had as much appeal to students of good ability as did the universities. Information on the kinds of students recruited for different institutions, by class, gender and school records seems an essential minimum for future planning of upper secondary and higher education. Studies might be both cross-sectional and longitudinal. Where such studies already exist they could usefully contribute to the evaluation of developing policies.

Secondly, and more difficult, it seems essential that both the local authorities and the Ministry have qualitative knowledge of how schools work. Part of this information might be, indeed, quantitative so that some idea of the distribution of teacher competences in relation to the working of the *Mønsterplan* could be elaborated. Does Norway know how many teachers are competent to teach mathematics at the different levels, for example? But a repertoire of cases on how schools now work would be particularly important. How do they fare under decentralisation? To what extent are they able to generate their own objectives within those of the national schemes? What organisational structures do they adopt in terms of disciplinary as against other kinds of school structures, including those concerned with pastoral and guidance work? Are the patterns of leadership managerial or collegial or mixtures? How far are schools able to respond to the need to co-operate with parents? What is the role of parents in expressing needs to the professionals? This kind of knowledge seems essential if schools are to be held accountable to the local authority and to Parliament. Moreover, Norway ought to want to disseminate knowledge of good practice and encourage its use as an example.

To enhance dissemination and the build up of a central evaluation and information system on the progress of education, Norway's high level of computerisation could be exploited, through the use of on-line networks between central, regional and local authorities and individual schools. Through these means, distance learning and the aggregation of administrative data could be advanced.

On the basis of both quantitative and qualitative information there could be active evaluation and monitoring of what the schools do. Some of the monitoring might be in the form of tests. Here we share the cautions of Norwegian policy-makers in imposing tests on the schools. It is, indeed, a matter of preference whether anxiety about standards should lead to elaborate systems of testing which might give certainty about the standards reached but which will also have backwash effects on the quality of education; teachers will then inevitably teach to the test and it has been remarked that there are more bad creators of tests than there are bad students. But shallow sample testing, which would enable the national authorities to have some idea of the state of knowledge throughout Norwegian schools, without identifying pupils or schools, could be a valuable diagnostic tool if mounted carefully. Moreover, Norway cannot avoid the question of whether other forms of monitoring ought not to be available. Other countries have inspectors and advisers who can help the schools engage in self-criticism and at the same time build up a picture for national use of the ways in which schools are progressing. Such evaluation would be primarily for development and information rather than for central control although it would, of course, also be available for investigating serious weaknesses.

In considering how evaluation might be made a strong component of Norwegian education, it is necessary to think in terms of the objectives of evaluation and then of the authority with which it shall be endowed and the technical characteristics of different forms of it.

The monitoring and evaluation functions seem largely absent from the reformed Norwegian system of education. As we have indicated earlier, a move from a centralised system cannot mean that the central ministries simply abandon the national stage. They remain to allocate resources, to create and administer the law, and to ensure that curriculum change is legislated and implemented. In order to perform these functions adequately, and to take a central role in continuing development of the system within the frameworks agreed in Parliament, they will certainly have to adopt an evaluative and monitoring function.

Equally, local authorities have a political responsibility for the maintenance of their schools and for the distribution of resources to them. But, as we have indicated, we believe there should also be a strong educational leadership function which will ensure that the schools are fully supported professionally but are also reviewed by a sympathetic but authoritative external body.

As far as the schools are concerned we would hope that they will develop a strong practice of self-critique and self-evaluation and at the same time will be able to seek help from external evaluation.

In brief, we are concerned not with the reintroduction of national controls but with considering ways in which good norms of educational practice can be established and disseminated better in Norway. Good practice needs to be identified and disseminated. The processes of education as well as its outcomes need to be considered. At present the analysis is likely to be that wholly of inputs which are important in themselves but give no good clue of what in fact is happening in Norwegian education.

The role of the regional director

With decentralisation, the role of the regional directors has changed. They are now the link between central government and the regions and the municipalities. Their control functions over, for example, the appointment of teachers has now gone and they are seeking to establish themselves, with relatively small staffs, as a training and advisory force. They have no power to evaluate the work of the schools. They provide information of a non-evaluative kind for the school boards. They have some influence in providing information about developments being worked out in the Ministry for teacher training colleges on leadership training. Their role could be strengthened to fulfill some of the activities suggested above.

The Advisory Councils

The Royal Ministry of Church and Education has not laid claim to competence in determining the substance of education and relies upon Advisory Councils to provide it with guidance on educational matters from the perspective of different sectors of the system. In principle, it must be right to have central institutions which are independent of the Ministry, which can be expert in their judgements, but yet uncluttered by the exercise of authority; they can be more flexible because they are not directly tied to the chariot wheels of the State.

As we have implied earlier, there is always a danger that such Advisory Councils will acquire different kinds of authority which will lead them to lose flexibility. Advice in principle is rendering a service which can be ignored, but if authoritative and not in competition with other sources of advice, it can take on the characteristics of a closed system. The present advisory system was built up in the times of centralisation and it may, therefore, need to face a period of adaptation to an era when local authorities and schools and their client groups will be moving into more powerful vantage points.

The *Mønsterplan* has been changed to allow for greater freedom in the schools. This, then, places a greater responsibility on the Advisory Councils to help the schools exercise their new discretion. The Advisory Councils follow the existing format of the education system and relate to such main structures as the primary and lower secondary schools and the upper secondary schools and vocational schools. But it might be considered sensible for the structure to be reconsidered in the light of the new tasks facing it. To follow the structure of the main sectoral boundaries assumes that existing boundaries between, for example, the vocational and general education of the secondary school and the administrative boundaries between upper and lower secondary school are correctly placed. They should themselves consider, therefore, whether there is enough room left in their work for cross-sectoral issues such as institutional development, the relationships between teacher professionalism and the stronger management by local authorities, and the place of parents and other clients in the school system.

The Advisory Councils play an important role in a system which has no professional educational expertise in the central ministries. They advise on the content of the *Mønsterplan*, on such issues as streaming, on decentralisation and leadership issues. But their role is uncertain in the new alignment of forces and Ministers are considering what part they might play.

The complexity of their work can be judged from the fact that the Advisory Council appointed by the Upper Secondary Board has to contend with 500 different courses, convenes 149 groups on examination questions and runs nearly 60 curriculum schools to look to them for advice.

We have already noted that, in part associated with the 1987 *Mønsterplan*, the Council for Primary and Lower Secondary Education has sponsored 3 000 locally-initiated development projects. The Councils record such projects, but they are locally initiated and mainly funded through the school directors who report to the Ministry. This seems to be an admirable initiative and likely to contribute to the growing strength and capacity for self-reflection in the schools. There are always, however, problems in securing the evaluation of local projects and the take-up and dissemination of their results in the schools. Because there is no central evaluation or monitoring capacity, it is not clear how the Advisory Councils' initiatives affect central policy-making and are taken in those schools which do not take part in the experiments.

The Local Authority Association

The Local Authority Association seems likely to step into the gap left by the divestation of power from the centre and its transfer to the local authorities. In our discussions with them, we were impressed by the way in which they had taken grip of a wide range of issues affecting local authorities.

It is their intention to bring the local authorities together into consortium relationships for a large number of developmental projects.

These in themselves are healthy developments but do not dispose of the question which we have tried to raise, namely, of the power that the centre must retain. Their position has certainly become far more central. They will negotiate salaries. If the national authorities do not build up resources of information and evaluation the Association will almost certainly fill the gap. Their contribution to evaluation and the collecting and dissemination of evaluation will be central, as we have suggested in our table. The problem will be to ensure that there is an agreed balance between the centre and the newly strengthened local authorities.

EVALUATION AND FOLLOW-UP AT DIFFERENT LEVELS OF THE SYSTEM

Objectives	Institutions and their tasks	Technical approaches to evaluation
Central ministries and development of national policy	Use of Advisory Councils for evaluating their sectors and making cross-sector evaluations, both to be linked to development work	Quantitative. Thin sampling of schools to build up picture of state education in major subject areas
	Creation of a national evaluation centre for the collation of national data and offering consultative service in the use of evaluative techniques	Longitudinal studies of pupils going through the system showing differential progress in different regions and types of schools, differential access to higher education and job destinations
	Use of regional directorates in a monitoring and evaluative role. Use of thin sampling of educational performance in key curriculum areas	Qualitative studies on the development of institutions, their responsiveness to external influences and client groups, relationships with parents, leadership patterns and the like
Local authorities' use of resources; implementation of reforms; and assistance to schools	Use of own professional staff to evaluate quality of education and to assess needs; ability to bring in external inspectors or advisers, including regional directors	Evaluating the outcomes of distribution of resources. Assessing quality of education given in schools. Rendering assurance to schools in self-evaluation
Schools' self-evaluation and rendering account to local authorities and client groups	Teachers themselves to conduct self-evaluation, possibly by use of peer groups within and outside the schools	Mainly qualitative measures of self-assessment
	Right to seek external evaluation and help	
	To be subject to evaluation by local authority and form part of thin sample of evaluation by national authorities	

VI

CRITICAL PERSPECTIVES AND PROPOSALS

Resource constraints on the achievement of objectives

In Chapter I we pointed out that the predicted changes in the economy and the demographic trends endorse the need for continued reform and evaluation of the education system to take account of the shift in climate. In particular, there is need to accept that the Norwegian public sector is likely to receive fewer rather than more resources as the revenues from oil recede.

We have had much to say about aspects of governance and decentralisation because of their importance in their own right but also because they vitally affect the capacity of the system to produce education of quality which will also respond to Norwegian social policy. Ultimately, our concern is with the style and quality of Norwegian education in all of its levels and questions of structure are subordinate to those overriding issues.

In this chapter we bring together the main areas of concern for consideration by the Norwegian authorities.

THE ROLE OF GOVERNMENT AND ECONOMIC CIRCUMSTANCES

The economy and central policy

Norwegian policy is the product of many admirable traditions. The respect for local and quite small groups in the society reflects itself in the multiplicity of local authorities, ministries, political parties and trade unions. In the past, it may have been possible to accommodate all of these interests because of two main factors. First, there has been consensus, which still largely obtains, about the aims of Norwegian educational policy. Common understandings reduce the arena for conflict or enforced negotiation and this has made smoother the policy-making process. Secondly, with the substantial lengthening of school life to include upper secondary education for the majority, and with the expansion of higher education, resource issues would have become sharp much earlier if oil wealth had not lubricated the system and made conflict over resources unnecessary. Generosity to the small units has always characterised Norwegian policy but has been possible to sustain because Norway has had resources to spare on its public sector.

As we have implied throughout this report, however, consensus and newly found wealth to meet newly agreed objectives have made it perhaps too easy for rational planning and purposeful development to remain in the background. Instead, the State has been able to satisfy itself that all is going reasonably well in terms of some of the assumptions derived from a more traditional era, whilst at the same time it has made ambitious reforms.

But the change in the contextual factors related in Chapter II, and our critique of the decentralisation plans, the relationships between different levels of governance, the relative weakness of perception of the role of higher education, all point to the need for a central developmental surge which will ride with, encourage and make good the objectives of modernisation, decentralisation and the further release from control of the prime institutions, namely the schools, colleges and universities.

We do not feel that there is anything inherent in Norwegian national values that negates the need to exercise political will decisively in the interests of the modernisation programme. Administrative rationality in this case involves clarifying the means to pursue the agreed ends of Norwegian policy. The clarification may reveal conflicts. For example, we are not certain that a prolific dispersal of power and of resources will be compatible with the reinforcement of equality. Equality is inseparable from quality. For quality to be safeguarded there has to be a strongly informed, well analysed and well expressed central view on what constitutes good institutions, effective planning at the local authority level and good monitoring and evaluation for the nation as a whole.

LOCAL GOVERNMENT

In Chapter V we gave our view of the structure of local government as it affects educational policy-making. We need only repeat, as part of what we have said about developing rationality and exercising political will, that there is a danger of balkanisation which needs to be tackled resolutely, even though we accept that politically this will be unpopular. The object will not here be to reduce the ability of institutions and local authorities to set their own styles and values. Just the contrary; weak and small local authorities will not be able to carry the enormous burdens involved in changing values, changing technical content and changing techniques in modern education.

USE OF RESOURCES

The examiners did not find it easy to comment on the use of educational resources because data about them were almost completely absent. Certain *prima facie* indications implied that a more rigorous analysis of resource use would yield profitable results; for example, the proliferation of a large number of small municipal local authorities; of small educational units at both the school and higher level; and the retention of single-purpose higher education institutions.

DATA AND EVALUATION

The data base

Norwegian education is not cheap; expenses per pupil are high and that is no doubt explained in part by geographical factors and the assumed necessity of maintaining a large number of local authorities and institutions in terms of the population being served.

The central authorities themselves feel that they do not have a strong data base upon which to make judgements of cost or effectiveness of the system. It is not possible to analyse costs and then link them to any analysis of outcomes, always a difficult task but rendered the more difficult when the information is not available. Anxiety about educational outcomes has already been noted. That anxiety is compounded by anxiety about what the schools are doing, what the outcomes are, in relationship to costs.

The transfer of funding from specific to general grants made to the local authorities will make it all the more difficult for the centre to know how public money is being spent.

Financial and other economic data about the system are necessary for good government. So, too, is strong research and development which can range over the whole area of policy concerns. The Research Council for Science and Humanities already funds a powerful and authoritative Institute for Studies in Research and Higher Education whose terms of reference, and many of whose studies, are directly relevant to policy development. There is no equivalent for the schools and we noted how the products of educational research were virtually absent in the national authorities' statement to the examiners. We understand that a Centre for Educational Research is being contemplated and we hope that such a centre may make a strong contribution to policy-making at the centre and in the local authorities and practice in the schools. The extent to which researchers' findings directly affect policy-making is always uncertain but we feel that Norway is ripe for a major effort in systematic and professional research on the very large policy arena of the schools.

In examining international data, we were surprised by the absence of material which could be useful to the Norwegian authorities for their own planning system.

Monitoring and evaluation at different levels

As noted in Chapter V the monitoring and evaluation functions seem largely absent from the reformed Norwegian system of education. As we have indicated earlier, a move from a centralised system cannot mean that the central ministries simply abandon the national stage. They remain to allocate resources, to create and administer the law, and to ensure that curriculum change is legislated and implemented. In order to perform these functions adequately, and to take a central role in continuing development of the system within the frameworks agreed in Parliament, they will certainly have to adopt an evaluative and monitoring function.

Equally, local authorities have a political responsibility for the maintenance of their schools and for the distribution of resources to them. But, as we have indicated, we believe there should also be a strong educational leadership function which will ensure that the schools are fully supported professionally but are also reviewed by a sympathetic but authoritative external body.

As far as the schools are concerned we would hope that they will develop a strong practice of self-critique and self-evaluation and at the same time will be able to seek help from external evaluation.

THE SCHOOL SYSTEM

The schools

The educational reforms are attempting to create enormous changes in the schools. Proposals for the extension of schooling down to the age of six, possibly through the greater incorporation of the kindergartens into the education system, and their expansion will further extend the range of education, the process well begun in the establishment of the common upper secondary school.

The problems that remain are not so much of provision and structure as of generating degrees of independence and strong professionalism within the schools. As we have stated in earlier sections, this will involve the extension of self-improvement projects, beyond the 3 000 already started, the expansion of the school leadership programme, the maintenance of an already ambitious in-service training programme, so that teachers will be better equipped to make their schools the centres of curriculum development and of relationships with the wider community.

We also believe that bringing in parents needs to be maintained but that an analysis of the formal power allocated to parental groups will also be necessary if this largely untapped resource is to be made available to the schools.

The 1987 *Mønsterplan* paves the way for a stronger teacher contribution towards the better running of the schools. This being so, society will increasingly believe that it is for teachers to maintain and advance the standards of education now that they have the freedom to do so. The improvement of the schools touches on the proposals for self-evaluation and monitoring discussed above.

Higher education

In Chapter IV we referred to the need to remandate higher education, and particularly the universities. We noted, too, that the regional colleges had developed well but raised questions about the proliferation of very small higher education institutions throughout the country and the uncertainty about their distribution of research functions between the universities and other institutions.

We further felt that whilst the relative separation of universities from the rest had enabled the regional colleges and other institutions to develop in their own way, there does now seem to be a need to relate the different parts of higher education into an integrated if loose-coupled system. Thus the universities ought to be more secure in their role of helping to train the teachers for the rest of the higher education system, particularly since non-university institutions will plainly develop further their role in applied research and development. Measures of integration are already well advanced inasmuch as students may transfer from one kind of institution to another.

At the same time, the relationship between universities and the non-university research institutes needs to be further considered. On the face of it, whilst a competitive structure has its merits, particularly when universities are reluctant to move into new and applied fields, the connection between research and teaching within the higher education and R&D nexus should not be lost.

We understand that the Hernes Commission will be taking up many of these issues.

EDUCATION AND THE LABOUR MARKET

We expressed earlier the belief that there was scope for developing the links between the labour market and the education sector. We were told of the mismatch between the needs of industry and education, that the upper stages of education were underequipped for their tasks and that teachers were behind industry in their knowledge. We were also advised that a transfer of education to the work place would be advantageous. The problem, which applied to higher education as well, was not simply a matter of resources but of curriculum emphasis and commitment. Skilled training was given a lower priority than general areas of education. The flow of engineers was insufficient to meet the needs. These views were shared by both employers and trade unionists whom we met.

More joint involvement and increased contacts between education and production enterprises in tackling specific needs and issues would be an example of development which might help bridge the gap. In the course of our review we visited some interesting examples of such joint involvement but such cases did not appear to be widespread. Instead our impression – reinforced by many of the views expressed – was that the educational sector is rather divorced from the activities of firms and the actual needs of the labour market. From this educational perspective private sector developments are often seen as simply creating problems, by spiriting away students and teaching staff.

Closer co-operation and greater mutual appreciation of each other's needs and objectives could improve the speed and effectiveness with which the educational sector adapts to the changing environment in which economic activity takes place. Greater co-operation could arise in a specific response to the needs for qualified personnel. Apart from attracting staff by offering higher salaries, employers could be encouraged to offer scholarships or pre-employment with release for recruits to take up specified courses of study. For their part staff might play a more active role in helping to meet the needs of industry both by way of greater involvement in applied research and in supplying advisory/consultancy services.

A further possibility relates to the links between the latter years of secondary education and initial employer needs in place of the extensive range of study options now offered. A more effective link could be created by placing more emphasis on the provision of basic language and mathematical skills and attempting less within the schools in the provision of specifically employment-orientated education. Here delicate choices have to be made and fashioned for local conditions. Small schools in remote areas, for example, will almost certainly lack specialist teachers and equipment for employment-related work. Moreover, it assumes an intimate dependency of school-leavers on what might be quite small local industry. If firms close or leave the area, the preparation in the schools will have proved to have been too specialist. At the same time, however, the balance between ensuring strong general education and making sure that the skills transferable to the world of working life are provided must be struck. Obviously, the more specific and direct links will occur more appropriately at the upper secondary level although even in the lower secondary stages pupils might be informed and receive preliminary initiations to the world of work.

ADULT AND SPECIAL EDUCATION

Adult education

We have noted that adult education, mostly provided by voluntary bodies, has gone through a period of reduced national support which may have affected its ability to recruit participants but that government has recently decided to increase its financial support. Its potential contribution, however, to policies of equality, regional distribution of educational opportunity and to training for work should safeguard its place in national policies. Links and exchanges with the formal system of education could be further developed. What place do the authorities see for adult education, including that provided by voluntary bodies, in strengthening the policies of equality and vocational education? How is it to be related to the provision made by local authorities?

Special education

In Chapter III we noted the gaps between strong policy intentions to integrate the education of children needing special provision with that of the rest of their age group and the practical difficulties, including some reluctance on the part of teachers and parents, to implement the 1975 law. Do the authorities intend to monitor the local authorities' interpretation of the 1975 law in view of these criticisms? Is provision in both initial and in-service training of teachers adequate to secure the implementation of policy?

TEACHER TRAINING AND RECRUITMENT

The quality and content of teacher training closely affect the ability of the Norwegian system to meet and to exploit fruitfully the changes in policy and in environment within which education is offered. We noted earlier that there is a link between the status of teachers, the ways in which they are recruited and trained, the salaries and conditions which they can then secure, and the views of the rest of society about the quality and status which should be accorded to them.

A Royal Commission is considering the future of teacher training and now does seem, indeed, to be exactly the right time to reappraise it as the effects of the reforms are being felt in the schools.

There seem to be causes for dissatisfaction with the present arrangements. In particular, students spend small amounts of time on a range of ten subjects. They spend half a year, one-sixth of their course, on professional training but the connections between practical work and their theoretical training are not always thought to be adequate.

We also noted earlier the lack of study of the distribution of teachers with various qualifications.

EQUALITY

We have referred to the Norwegian tradition of equality and the great steps taken to achieve it. We noted how the movement from equality of opportunity has moved towards more positive attempts, through the distribution of higher and upper secondary education throughout the country, for example, and in the provision for minority groups.

We expressed the view that measures of social engineering are essential to establish the framework, but that these essentially input measures are only effective if rigorous attention is paid to the processes and outcomes of education. In reducing generalised objectives for education to their particulars, teachers will fulfill the egalitarian creed only if they fully assess each child for his needs and make sure that the pedagogical systems offer the particular educational patterns that individuals need. We were left uncertain that Norwegian teacher education and the system for in-service training was fully equipping teachers for these difficult professional tasks.

We also felt that deference to localism can produce ambiguous outcomes in terms of equality. If the school or college is near the home, access is more possible. But what is provided is then likely to be in a small institution not able to provide the specialist resources for advanced study. We emphasize, therefore, that the full interpretation of equality means equal opportunity to the highest quality of education as well as to the wide distribution of educational opportunities. In the same cause, we have criticised the existence of a plethora of very small local education authorities which may not be able to provide the in-service facilities, the equipment and the access to high-level education that is more possible in greater concentrations of resources.

Do the authorities share the examiners' view of the links between quality and equality of education, to be achieved through increased individualisation of needs assessment and of teaching and learning processes? Would a more explicit sharing of power between teachers and parents strengthen this process?

Do the authorities accept that the drive towards decentralisation, and the maintenance of small units of administration and education might affect the possibility of high-quality education delivered equally to all Norwegians?

CONCLUSION: STRENGTHENING THE SYSTEM AT ALL OF ITS LEVELS

We have not spared our criticisms of a system which has much cause for self-congratulation. Although some of the schools and higher education institutions are said to be poorly housed and equipped – and we could not form a view of this – a great deal of money and other resources have been put into the education system since the last OECD review on

Norway. The traditional mould has been broken through a powerful thrust towards decentralisation from a hitherto regulatory centre. Higher education has increased its access, particularly for women, and if not amongst the highest in the international league in terms of the proportion of young people seeking places in it, it has created the remarkable system of regional colleges which have been able to secure a degree of parity of esteem with the universities.

Throughout all of this, Norwegian values of power for the people in their home localities, a universal belief in the state school system as opposed to private institutions, an innate belief in equality, have all informed what can be described as the massive social engineering of recent educational policy.

The next stage of reform will move the focus from major changes in the system to improving the quality of what the system produces. Of all of the reforms, the 1987 *Mønsterplan*, in encouraging schools to apply the curriculum in terms not only of the national frame but also in terms of their own local needs will be the most difficult to establish. It will involve a major shift in teacher assumptions and in working practices. But we salute the effort.

In making our recommendations for change, which particularly concern the structure of the centre in relationship to the localities, the organisation of the localities themselves and a new mandate for higher education, we have not sought to weaken any of the components. We do not believe that there is a finite amount of authority, power and influence that can be exercised. This is not a zero-sum game. We believe that the ministries, in relinquishing their earlier and more traditional forms of power, should generate new forms of influence through the power of knowledge, the ability to collate and to disseminate news of good practice, and to sustain a critical and evaluative eye on the whole system. That will be a stronger role than is created by the administration of detailed and perhaps archaic restrictions and rules.

In suggesting that the proliferation of local authorities must mean weak instruments of national and local policy, we share the views of Norwegians that the local voice should be strong. We argue for a one-tier system of regions although we know that local authority will be more remote from the basic institutions than are many municipal authorities at present. But the region will itself be a more competent and professional institution able to take both a strategic and a supporting role. And the removal of the small local authority close to the school will enable the school itself to develop degrees of self-confidence and autonomy which must amount to stronger professionalism in the work that it does.

Equally, we do not suggest that universities should be given more freedom simply for the sake of academic self-indulgence. A free society needs free institutions but in securing their mandate they must become aware, as are many universities throughout the world now, of the fact that they exist within an exchange relationship with the rest of society. Society will only legitimise them and give them funds if there is a good return for the resources and their privileges. They should be strong enough to generate their own income but at the same time have degrees of freedom conferred through state monies. They should be free to pursue basic research and critical enquiry but at the same time adopt an active view of social and economic needs. The distinction between applied and basic research is less one of intellectual content and of knowledge rules than of who sets the objectives for research and development. We suggest that these matters are negotiable between sponsors and sponsored, and that the universities cannot wait much longer before engaging in the State to secure a refreshment and realignment of their social mandate.

If the universities become strong in both their independence and their interdependence with other social institutions, including the State, so can the regional and other colleges begin to sketch out more firmly their role as teachers of the majority of those who leave school and as institutions capable of helping their localities in different forms of advanced training and applied research and development.

A clear definition of policies, of the processes of policy-making and of the different roles in Norwegian educational policy-making will, therefore, be designed to cut nobody down to size but to build all of the relevant institutions up to their appropriate size and strength.

The objectives of Norwegian education seem to us to be wholly appropriate and we believe that those elements in need of reform which are essentially structural and institutional can be more closely aligned to the objectives which they are intended to serve. That will present a stimulating challenge for the central authorities and for all who are concerned with the further advancement of Norwegian education.

Part Two

RECORD OF THE REVIEW MEETING

Paris, 28 May 1988

The Chairman, *Mr. Hummeluhr*, said that the Education Committee were grateful to the Norwegian Government and the team of examiners for presenting excellent reports which touched upon many of the key matters that were already engaging the attention of the Committee. Such issues as evaluation and monitoring, higher education, its role and development, the conditions and work of teachers, were all part of their continuing agenda.

Mrs. Grøndahl, the Norwegian Minister of Church and Education, began by congratulating Mr. Hummeluhr on his election as Chairman of the Committee. She continued:

"On behalf of the Norwegian government I would like to thank the OECD for the opportunity which they have given us to have the results of our national educational policy scrutinised both by outstanding international educational experts and by your good selves, members of this select Committee.

I would like to thank the examiners for their frank report – for pointing out areas which they feel need closer attention and special items which evidently should be reviewed.

Some of the areas we were perhaps aware of as sore points. An education system is, however, like a process. No government can start afresh. Tradition, and not least groups with vested interests, mean that things do not change that fast.

I thank you all in advance for this unique opportunity to discuss the development of the Norwegian education system. The fruits of your work will be evident in the future schooling of Norwegian youth.

THE BACKGROUND REPORT

I will briefly turn to our Background Report where we have tried to stress the areas which we feel are of the greatest importance and which would also apply to an international audience facing rather similar situations.

Adaptation of education to all

The equal rights for everyone to receive tuition and be part of an educational society are recognised by all parties. In the comprehensive school we accept nearly all children within the ordinary classrooms and try to meet those who have special needs with assistance in their local surroundings. In the upper secondary schools, pupils needing adapted tuition are actually given priority of admission and the tuition aims to be in accordance with the potential of the pupil.

Youth guarantee

To young people the right and opportunity of education and work are of the highest importance. Without specific legal guarantees the Norwegian society has been able to secure most young people under the age of 20 the possibility of a job or a place at school.

Lifelong education

My government is deeply concerned as regards the objectives of lifelong education. We all know that technology and modern industry move so fast that the process of new learning is a constant factor in our world of work. The increasing speed of technology has faced us with challenges of large proportions.

We still have large groups in working life who have not had such an opportunity. We feel it as our duty and a political necessity to extend the possibility of new learning to these large groups. This calls for an extensive programme as regards lifelong education.

THE NORWEGIAN LONG-TERM PROGRAMME

My government is at present preparing a revised long-term programme where we will draw up the aims of our policies for the 1990s. The programme is mainly based on the extensive change in the national economy. The new economic situation requires a change of priorities.

Education and development of competence at all levels will be of crucial importance in an offensive strategy for economic development and renewal of the welfare state. In this respect our main national objectives are:

- improvement of knowledge and competence
- lifelong education
- further promotion of equal right to education
- personal and democratic development.

Modern and new technology have great significance and impact upon our daily life. Some of the main tools in this struggle are to make the teaching profession attractive, to update teachers who for long periods have been away from the world of work and to introduce concrete plans for making vocational schools and teachers into resource centres for the main vocations in the districts.

In the long-term programme lifelong education is an overall objective for our education policy in general.

Strategy

Our strategy will be to draw all tiers into the efforts. We must clarify the responsibility at the regional levels, and the responsibility of the voluntary organisations, as well as the organisations of the world of work.

We must again review our laws and regulations in order to avoid putting decisions up to too high a level.

Both the Background and the Examiners' Reports deal with various problems in connection with decentralisation. I would like to point out that further decentralisation is hardly likely to be considered.

Main topics

From the various school categories I would like to stress the following points:
We feel a basic need to increase the level of knowledge and motivate pupils for better work.

We are aware that the school day for the youngest children is too short. An increase of the number of school days a year is considered as well as other organised activities during the week days.

We want the comprehensive school to be comprehensive where education and upbringing are seen in a total context. The kindergarten, the after-school child care and the comprehensive school ought to co-operate to a greater extent.

An educational alternative for all six-year-olds ought to be developed. The alternative ought to be placed at the school, based on pedagogical ideas adapted to this group.

We are also planning greater freedom for the school unit within a specified framework.

A crucial question is the balance between the role of the teacher as the traditional teacher and as part of a team, responsible for the child for the greater part of the day.

For the upper secondary school we have under review whether the number of options ought to be more limited and thus make the decision of the students easier. We are also contemplating whether it would be an advantage that the initial year should be the same for all students in the same areas of study.

At present, the right of enrolment in a university is limited to students of the general and economic and clerical areas of study. We are considering extending this right of enrolment further to the vocational areas, provided the students attend an extra period of schooling.

We aim at building up improved competence in the world of work through adult education, to improve vocational education and further integration between vocational and general education.

My ministry is now preparing three white papers on these aims to be presented to Parliament in the spring of 1989 in connection with our long-term programme.

Higher education

As regards higher education, the OECD review comes at a stage when we have an abundance of questions, while we are somewhat reluctant to provide definite answers. A main reason for this is the work of a Royal Commission on Higher Education, scheduled to present its report in the early autumn. The Examiners' Report is a valuable input into the work of the Commission but, as you will understand, we are not in a position to reply to the questions of the examiners on the basis of the Commission's proposals.

However, some essential policy directions are already fairly clear. The universities have lately received and will get even more freedom to run their own affairs. On the other hand, the ministry may become stricter in its budgetary preference for institutions proving their capability of handling their own affairs.

The fundamental reform of the 1970s, the development of a system of regional colleges, has proved a major success, in many respects. The future task is to strengthen the coordination of smaller institutions at the regional level, and to develop further their links with the universities, without endangering the specific mission of the college system. Regional development concerns will still figure strongly in educational policies at this level. However, this should be a balanced development not yielding to tendencies towards even more small institutions, and aspirations towards longer studies in the regions.

Demographic developments make it necessary to have an even stronger emphasis on adult and continuing education also at the tertiary level. We may have to look forward to some central mechanism – call it an open university if you wish – which could co-ordinate the efforts in this field by higher education institutions and adult education organisations, as well as the public library system. This we must do in order to obtain the professional authority and the financial strength necessary for extensive developmental work and the purchase of high-quality services from existing institutions and organisations. We might end up with an organisation like this serving as our fifth university, which could also be seen as an instrument for qualitative upgrading of the smaller institutions in a very decentralised system.

I will end this statement, Mr. Chairman, with thanking you for your attention. We look forward to your various comments."

I

RESOURCE CONSTRAINTS ON THE ACHIEVEMENT OF OBJECTIVES

Professor O'Donoghue, on behalf of the examiners, said how much they had welcomed the opportunity to study the system. It was a remarkable experience to be able to note the changes that had taken place over the years. The examiners had seen it as their function to make a positive contribution in accordance with the purposes of the reviews, namely, to give OECD countries an opportunity to learn from each other's experiences. In studying the unique characteristics of other systems we come to understand more fully the nature of our own. In fulfilling their mission, the examiners benefited from the warm co-operation, hospitality and understanding of their Norwegian hosts.

The meeting then began to consider the issues raised by the examiners in Chapter VI of their report. Prof. O'Donoghue said that in common with other OECD countries, Norway had been going through a period of economic readjustment over the last few years, a process likely to continue. It seemed from the many economic surveys conducted by the OECD that most of the Norwegian adjustment would be represented by increasingly tight control on public expenditure, by both central and local government.

Since the time of the previous Norwegian review in 1974, the education system had developed considerably. The country report contained proposals for further improvement and expansion; increases in kindergarten and early schooling, further expansion at the upper secondary level, and for more recurrent teacher training, with the development of special regional centres to cater for it, the proposals from regional colleges to further develop, all of these spoke to the desire for further development. Other financial pressures were mounting, including demands for improved remuneration for teachers.

Question 1

Do the Norwegian authorities feel it possible to meet their objectives within the changing economic and demographic framework?

It was noticeable that many of the pressures derived from the increased activities of the regional and local authorities. This would lead to the discussion, later in the session, of the relationships between central and local government.

Mrs. Grøndahl said that the maintenance of full employment had been the principal objective of Norwegian policy, and that had been successfully achieved. As a result there had indeed been pressure for highly-qualified labour and that had contributed towards a shortage of teachers in the schools. Full employment had been possible because of the decision to limit private consumption whilst at the same time maintaining public expenditure. It was now accepted that some curbing of public expenditure might be necessary although they nonetheless aimed for further increases in the level of enrolment to the different stages of admission. They believed that there was untapped expertise in the school system which could be used better and they thus looked for a higher degree of effectiveness in the use of resources. They intended, in spite of possible economic constraints, to substantially increase the role of adult education, to look most keenly at ways of improving the system through evaluation, of adding to its efficiency through the use of computers and in-service education and training of teachers, and to open up the school to parents and to its immediate environment.

Mr. Bakke, Minister of Cultural and Scientific Affairs, accepted that the economy might now present difficulties but the Norwegian government had no intention of changing its policies of development. Indeed, there were opportunities to improve education without additional expenditure because whilst the number of teachers had been increased, there was now a reduction in the number of pupils going through the system. There was strong popular and political support for education in Norway. The question being asked was not whether Norway spends too much but whether the resulting education was good enough. Decentralisation was partly predetermined by Norwegian geography. It was not a luxury to be afforded in good times and to be done away with when times become harder. Decentralisation was important not only educationally but also in a social and economic context. No great changes would be made but the system will be improved. The local authorities had recently been given their autonomy; the examiners' points about the need for stronger evaluation were well taken. The system must be effectively monitored.

Mr. Papadopoulos (OECD Secretariat) asked whether decentralisation, so far from adding to the cost, might not introduce new and different resources from the local communities which might not otherwise be available to education. *Mr. Bakke* replied that that was precisely the purpose of decentralisation. By moving decision-making nearer the people the Norwegian authorities were inviting stronger involvement in education.

Moreover, they were not convinced that decentralisation was in itself more expensive. There was no evidence that economies of scale could be secured, particularly in view of the geographical distribution in Norway.

II

THE ROLE OF CENTRAL GOVERNMENT AND THE LOCAL AUTHORITIES

Prof. Kogan introduced the following questions:

Question 2

Are the central authorities satisfied that, given the ambitious drive towards decentralisation, and the maintenance of small administrative units, they have retained sufficient involvement in the shaping of policy and the sufficient analytic support which this would require?

The Norwegian authorities had deliberately moved from the certainties of traditional democratic forms of government towards the uncertainties of strong local democracy. It was a leading example of the increased attempts at devolution within OECD countries, with the deviant example of the United Kingdom excepted.

The Norwegian authorities had stated that devolution might not cost more, particularly since there were more teachers and fewer pupils in the school system. But the issue was not one of cash costs but rather whether the costs, at whatever level, were producing an appropriate quality of education. It was not only a matter of money. It could also be asked whether in return for increased power in the communities they would deliver better education. Both of these questions could be answered only if there were strong and sensitive evaluative arrangements.

A further question resulting from the drive towards decentralisation was: *what would now be the role of the Norwegian central authorities?* Norway has moved from the traditional to the second and decentralised model of democratic government. But devolution did not emancipate government from responsibilities. The Minister's own agendas of what had to be done implied a strong and determined set of nationally-established objectives. But the central setting of objectives must depend upon good information about what was happening in the schools, and an ability to take action if the objectives were not being met. Would there be good arrangements enabling them to monitor and steer without using regulation and prescription?

Question 3

Are the authorities satisfied that the present two-tier system, and the small municipalities which it entails, will be capable of ensuring that the national objectives are met and that the schools will be sufficiently supported?

Question 4

How does the Ministry envisage its future relationships with the Advisory Councils, if it is accepted that the centre must adopt a stronger planning and informative role? Has it plans for the reactivation of the regional directorates to serve as advisers to the schools and local authorities and the evaluative agents of the centre?

Question 5

Can resources be used more rationally, given the desire to respect local autonomy and the need for geographical dispersal of facilities?

Prof. Kogan said that it must seem unlikely that very small communities would be able to provide the expertise that will be required for the very complex tasks that the schools will have to carry, particularly as increased devolution comes into effect and as they begin to apply the new *Mønsterplan*.

The examiners were concerned that there should be discontinuity between different stages of education. The transition between the different stages was always difficult but arrangements for it could be enhanced if the two levels of schooling were under the same direction.

Mrs. Grøndahl replied that they had total confidence in local authorities to provide excellent education for children. But there were important central aspects which should be recalled. Many projects for school development were undertaken within a central overview. They were resolved that devolution would be accompanied by a strengthening of evaluation throughout the system. It was the beginning of a process and it was difficult to fix criteria. The regional directors of the school system (referred to later) were able to report back on progress in the schools. There were 448 communities; there was, however, a continuing process of amalgamation and more was necessary. Local identities were strong and obstinate. There was, however, encouraging evidence of voluntary co-operation between communities in, for example, psychological services and in-service training.

They regarded the examiners' suggestion that comprehensive education might come under the counties rather than the communities as "unthinkable". It would not be possible within the Norwegian geographical setting for there to be sufficient contact between the schools and the more remote county systems.

The Chairman then enquired what might be the role of the regional director in creating co-operation. *Mrs. Grøndahl* replied that the regional director no longer had control functions. But he was able to help the school systems develop through arranging co-operative ventures and his reports would also ensure that the Ministry were informed about the running of the schools.

III

DATA AND EVALUATION, AND THEIR CONNECTION WITH DECENTRALISATION

Question 6

Would it be advisable to revise the structure for the collation and use of data, both quantitative and qualitative, for assessing and monitoring the progress of the system to assist all levels in their policy-making?

Question 7

Have the Norwegian authorities a view on how the evaluative functions analysed earlier in the report might be performed? How might functions be distributed between the Ministry, its regional directors, the Advisory Councils and the local authorities in securing evaluation, monitoring and self-development throughout the system?

Prof. Lundgren noted that Norway was moving from a "rule-governed system" to a "goal-governed system". This meant that goals must be more precise and visible. Otherwise the local school systems would not get adequate advice from the centre. Hernes and Olsen had observed that Norway had a rather overcrowded policy arena. This led to the creation of goals which were too abstract. One way out of the problem was to create a better information base on how the schools operated.

Such an information system needed to fulfill three different purposes. There was a need for basic information about the school system, a statistical base including knowledge about resource needs and use. This would have consequences for the organisation of the central authorities. Were there plans to reorganise the Advisory Councils, or to create a new council for this purpose?

Secondly, information about the quality of schools was needed. This would lead to the creation of indicators, perhaps based upon testing. These would be directed to seeing how far national goals were fulfilled. Was there the expertise to develop evaluation and the necessary test construction?

Thirdly, evaluation was a way of governing the school system. Any form of evaluation, testing or securing data from the schools implied the central authority's expectations of the schools. Was there any strategy which will link evaluation to development work?

Mrs. Grøndahl replied that she had no clear answers but the Norwegian authorities were determined to try to find them. They accepted that it was not possible to solve problems merely by putting in more money. Their policy would be to evaluate and to rationalise. They intended to extend development work which would also be a governing tool for the local authorities. They accepted that their statistical system was not too good but they were stepping it up in range and quality. They accepted that more research was needed and they had now instituted two programmes on management organisation and governing for the whole range of public administration, but with special reference to the school system. A Centre of Research in Education was being formed and they were trying to attract appropriate researchers in this field. They sought proposals on evaluation of the school system for researchers and this would go far beyond mere testing.

They had given thought to the role of the Advisory Councils and hoped to make them more effective. It was possible that they would be amalgamated into a single body for this purpose.

Mr. Knauss (Germany) noted that whilst Norway had increased its number of teachers and thus improved the staffing ratios, there were difficulties in getting highly-qualified teachers. There were also the problems of teacher salaries. Was there some connection between teacher supply and decentralisation? Were there national scales? Did the local communities have the opportunities to offer incentives?

Mr. Bréant (France) asked whether the regional directorate would be able to fulfill its new and delicate role with the same kind of staff or would there be changes in it. *Mrs. Grøndahl* replied that whilst each municipality hired its own teachers, and the county employed teachers for the upper secondary school, there was a state school scale. Soon, however, a joint county and municipality system would take over the negotiations with the teachers. There were no supplementary merit awards but remote district employment carried some supplement on the basis of a parliamentary decision. The problem about teachers' salaries was that there were many part-time women teachers who helped depress the general level.

She continued that the municipalities did not like the concept of the regional directorate as a powerful entity in the system. They were, however, engaging in some retraining for their new role and there would be some build-up of staff for it. *Mr. Bakke* said that it was difficult to keep the supply and demand for teachers in good balance. Three or four years ago they were abundant. With the decline in the number of students, a problem of oversupply might emerge. The local authorities had hired a large number of new teachers and that might cause problems, despite a declining number of pupils. Teachers left teaching and went to other areas of work. Was that a bad thing? Even Mr. Gorbachev thought that ten years in one job was enough. As long as it did not drain the school system of the people that were badly needed, some transfer to other occupations was surely desirable. Students still wanted to enter teachers' colleges. They were highly-qualified students. Teachers' colleges were well decentralised and that enabled recruitment to be efficient and for teachers recruited to remain for a long while in post.

Mr. Papadopoulos, returning to the question of evaluation, asked whether an inspectorate had been considered. He also understood that statistics were centralised so that there were none available directly under the control of the two Ministries.

Mrs. Grøndahl replied that they did not like the word "inspector" but they were keen, as had been stated, on developing other kinds of evaluation. (*Mr. Bakke* added that they had read the works of Gogol.) There were already some evaluative measures available as, for example, the examinations administrered centrally after the ninth grade and the end of upper secondary school. *Mrs. Grøndahl* added that they were now developing their own ministry statistics.

Question 8

Do the Norwegian authorities believe that arrangements made by both the centre and the local authorities will sufficiently encourage self-appraisal and other forms of development in the teaching profession?

Question 9

Will the upper secondary schools have sufficient resources to aim successfully for the multiple objectives stated for them? Is the current process of updating likely to secure strong support from pupils and other groups such as employers for what they are doing?

Prof. Lundgren said that the questions might be reformulated. Decentralisation involved questions about the balance between political and professional governing. Degrees of decentralisation had always been present because of teacher power in the schools. Paradoxically, decentralisation would create a stronger frame within which teachers must work. There would be an increase in signals from both the central and the local authorities. Teachers would also be required to be more responsive to public debate about the quality of education.

But what incentives will be put into the system to encourage the teachers to involve themselves fully in these changes?

Mrs. Grøndahl replied that teachers would be able to move from relative personal isolation towards working on the curriculum in teams, a major change in the traditional role of teachers. They would also benefit from more intensive participation by parents. They intended to look to changes in the teachers' working day and to see what it amounted to when viewed from their programme over the whole year. Authorities must contribute to in-service training.

Mrs. Vohn (Denmark) said that decentralisation raised the question of the balance between quality and equality in education. Norway had always been a leader in equality. The Education Committee had recently considered issues concerning gender equality in the school system. There were also proposals for the new adult education centre. What were the principles and goals that were being pursued?

Mr. Bréant (France), referring to Section II of the summary (see Part Three), noted that there seemed to be uncertainty about whether pupils were organised primarily by age or whether there was any form of streaming in the system. *Mrs. Grøndahl* replied that in basic education each pupil received an adapted education and there was no ranking. *Mrs. Grøndahl* and *Mr. Bakke* said that they were concerned with both quality and equality. Their attempts to improve quality were part of the effort to establish equality. These goals did not conflict with each other. By establishing equality the whole qualitative level of the system should be increased. But they were concerned that quality should be substantially improved throughout, especially in small schools. Improvements were particularly needed in the upper secondary school. They had made special efforts to improve gender equality even if girls were making very traditional choices. Where institutions were of similar quality the general level was higher.

Prof. Kogan said that the diffusion of education through equality increased the general level of the system. But two reservations should be noted. First, the emphasis on the locality in small units would make it difficult for more advanced work in upper secondary schools to be available in the way that it should be and could be in the urban centres. Parochial attitudes might also conflict with good quality education. People in the latter parts of schooling can be able and highly motivated given the right conditions. The upper secondary school was pulled by several kinds of locomotives. One was the democratic theme and Norway had been strong in democratising upper secondary education. Secondly, there was the need to ensure that upper secondary education was sensitive to the need for training for employment, although it should be noted that Norwegian employers said that they were not too well satisfied with their connections with upper secondary education. Thirdly, there was the incentive system established by higher education. But in Norway, because no particular status was attributed to any of the different forms of higher education, the upper secondary schools did not strain towards academic excellence in the way that could be found in other countries such as France or the United Kingdom. The democratic and labour market norms were being well attended to. The academic norms might well benefit from more attention.

Prof. O'Donoghue added that in thinking about the employment relationship with upper secondary education there was some need for ambiguity. It was important not to overdefine functions and relationships if social cohesion was not to be weakened.

Members of the Committee then took up several points relating to the school system. *Prof. Sette* (Italy) noted the importance of not confusing equality with uniformity. The function of education was to enhance the individual development of people. They would then contribute better to the economy and to society.

Mrs. Grøndahl said that the small upper secondary school units could work well if the counties ensured some co-ordination of provision between them. It was still difficult to hire fully-qualified teachers and to elaborate textbooks for the Sami population. *Mr. Neumüller* (Austria) noted the provision for Sami and other minorities education. Did Norwegian education also incorporate learning about the cultures of the minorities? *Mrs. Grøndahl* said that as many as 40 native tongues were taught in Oslo. There was provision for the teaching of Norwegian to those whose native tongue was otherwise and there was considerable provision for people to sustain their own native languages as well within the school system. *Prof. Sette* (Italy) noted the Norwegian determination, expressed in the 1974 review as well, to preserve local cultures and wondered whether this carried through to higher education and whether there were connections with other Nordic countries. *Mr. Ivič* (Yugoslavia) asked whether there were special schools or classes for gifted children. Were there adapted programmes and extra tuition and grants available for the most competent, especially for those opting for higher education? *Mrs. Grøndahl* replied that they did not make such provision but teachers were expected to apply particular attention to both those with special needs and also to gifted children. They were conscious of the need to maintain and support minority cultures and there was strong provision for the Sami people. There was a Sami Parliament and co-ordination with other Scandinavian countries.

IV

HIGHER EDUCATION

Attention then turned to questions on higher education:

Question 10

Do the Norwegian authorities believe that it will be possible to improve Norwegian higher education by the amalgamation, perhaps in federal systems, of the many small units of higher education and establish links more firmly between the universities and other institutions?

Question 11

Will it be possible to negotiate a social contract with higher education which will guarantee greater degrees of budgetary certainty and freedom on such matters as staffing establishments at the same time as the institutions, and particularly the universities, undertake to clarify their objectives in consultation with the public authorities?

Question 12

Is it possible as well to formulate plans that will ensure that the ablest students undertake the longer courses offered by the universities in order to ensure the future recruitment of competent people to the country's R&D system?

Prof. Kogan, introducing the questions, said that Norway provided a very particular example of the organisation of higher education. There was an "inverted binary system" in which, although there were distinctions between universities and other institutions of higher education, the status system was not strongly demarcated and, indeed, in some respects was reversed. In viewing Norwegian higher education one noted challenges to higher education which were to be found elsewhere: increased managerialism, the attempt to make higher education more efficient and responsive to the needs of society, and some depression amongst academic staff.

Turning to the questions, it was noted that the Hermes Commission would be looking to such issues as the amalgamation of small units of higher education. It was also noted from a statement by the Minister that there might be an arrangement, possibly to be thought of as a fifth university of an open-university type, which would establish links between regional colleges, adult education and other institutions of higher education. The many small units of higher education were often quite ambitious in maintaining that they were developing research programmes and programmes leading to the production of doctoral candidates. The examiners expressed doubts about such developments unless there were firmer linkages with the universities. But there was a problem in higher education in Norway which was difficult to analyse and express. Some areas of higher education expressed a sense of disenchantment reinforced by more tangible evidence. For example, the largest university in Norway was to some extent bypassed in terms of the country's courses. The pull of the labour market was too strong. There were strong preferences for regional teacher training colleges. Higher education's mandate, particularly for research and for the more academic functions, seemed to be relatively weak. The psychology and culture of higher education were thus questions to be pursued. The effects on the research system needed also to be considered.

Mr. Bakke stated that the Norwegian authorities shared the concerns of the examiners. They had appointed the Royal Commission to pursue many of them. It should be recognised that there was strong resistance from small units and their local politicians to amalgamation. They now needed to evaluate the role of the regional colleges. It was accepted that it was not sensible for small institutions conducting a limited range of functions to coexist, often quite near to each other. It was less certain whether simply loosening the budgetary strings would cause universities to flourish; the problem was more complex. There had been a loosening of controls but the universities seemed to find it difficult to exercise their freedom: they still asked questions of the Ministry that were unnecessary. One needed a change in the organisational culture of the universities. Were the governing systems appropriate? Was the leadership too academic? The regional college system recruited people to higher education who might not otherwise come. They could move on to the universities. They were then likely to go back to the region from which they came. That must be a good thing. But it was certainly true that more students needed to enter the longer courses. There was cause for anxiety about recruitment to research. There were now some scholarships for studies lasting more than five years. The number of research assistantships had been increased in the current financial year.

Mr. Morin (Netherlands) referred to the co-ordination of adult education as a form of open university. Were there proposals for the central development of such expensive materials as interactive media? Was there evaluation of such media? *Mr. Knauss* (Germany) asked what the problem was with the universities. Equipment or social status? What consequences were there? Did many Norwegian students prefer to study abroad? *Prof. O'Donoghue* noted how the regional colleges had had a salutary effect on the system. They had presented challenges to what could easily be a complacent university structure and offered competition and examples of change. *Prof. Kogan* said that in noting what Mr. Bakke said about needs for new management it was important that those concerned recognised multiple needs. It was important that higher education leaders should be good managers and that they should be able to be entrepreneurial in developing the resources of their institutions. But if they were not able to connect well with the academic purposes and activities of their institution, the quality of higher education would suffer.

Mr. Bakke replied that the universities' status had been affected by the breaking of their monopoly and regional colleges had diverted some investment from the universities. Some universities had been undernourished and needed more money now. At the same time the emphasis on research should be regulated carefully. Students complained that there was not enough attention to the teaching function of the university and it was important to encourage its improvement. *Mr. Riviere* (Spain) said that the Spanish authorities were considering how teachers for higher education might be selected so that the teaching function was given due weight. *Mr. Charters D'Azevedo* (Portugal) said that they had overcome the problem in Portugal to some extent by creating separate budgets for the training of university staff.

V

EDUCATION AND THE LABOUR MARKET

The following questions by the examiners were considered;

Question 13

Do the Norwegian authorities feel that connections between education and the labour market might be further strengthened, perhaps by offering more training in the work place during the latter periods of schooling?

Question 14

Are there sufficient contacts between education authorities at the different levels, teachers in schools, and employers? Are there ways of securing a stronger employers' contribution to education through student sponsorship, loans of equipment and the like?

Prof. O'Donoghue said that full employment created special demands on education. There was inevitably a conflict between education and the labour market as a whole in getting their share. The question that might be asked was, were the links good enough? The achievement of full employment meant that these tensions would be all the stronger. The perspectives of employers differed from those providing education. *Mr. Løken* (Norway) said that there was certainly a great deal more to be done in securing better conditions between the labour market and education. There were two routes. Young people could train for craftsmanship or vocational work through either the school or the apprenticeship system. Both were being tried in parallel. Apprenticeship systems could be based upon one year in the upper secondary school, or two years. Then the apprenticeship continued in employment. Or the whole bulk of the apprenticeship could be taken in the school. Norway tried to get joint responsibility for training in these ways. Even when most of the training took place in the school, perhaps for three years, six months were spent in employment. Some difficulties may arise from the fact that employers do not think too much of what goes on in the school and it is often difficult to get teachers trained in specialist areas. There were good connections between employers and education on the Advisory Councils for upper secondary school and on the Advisory Council for the functions of apprenticeship training. Attempts were made to recruit vocational teachers from industry. Most companies had fewer than 50 employees. The Ministry tried to encourage the exchange of equipment or machinery. The upper secondary school might then become the resource centre for employment training.

VI

THE UPPER SECONDARY SCHOOL

Mr. Knauss (Germany) raised questions about the upper secondary school. What was the rationale for having all of the streams in one institution? Were the reasons managerial? Was it because there was a common core of curriculum? What were the expectations of participation of young people in the upper secondary school? What proportions attended? Did all have the right of access to higher education after upper secondary school? How many went to the labour market? Do employers accept all of the different routes of access? To what extent do young people choose between upper secondary school or work or a combination?

The Minister replied that there was a strong belief in having upper secondary schools for all young people. Apart from democratic arguments, it was important that the theoretical and the practical should be seen to be well related. Young people were not sure what they wanted to do and the system ought therefore to be flexible, enabling them to make choices when they wanted to. There were issues about the number of different lines in upper secondary schools. But 90 per cent of all 16-year-olds entered them and they had increased the capacity to meet this. It had helped them to avoid youth unemployment. Of the whole age group, 20 per cent then continued to higher education. As Mr. Løken noted, it was possible for them to make a wide choice between ways in which they would prepare themselves for the labour market.

VII

SOME GENERAL POINTS

Mr. Charters D'Azevedo (Portugal) enquired how far there was co-operation between schools and work and whether computers were being introduced in the schools. How far did firms support the schools with new equipment and help provide technical teaching in the secondary schools?

Mrs. Grøndahl replied that there was a strong attempt to introduce computers into the schools. They had been concerned with the problems of the training of teachers and of introducing hardware. The main issue was now getting appropriate software and there were co-operative schemes between Nordic countries in this respect.

Mrs. Grøndahl also said that a paper was being presented by a Parliamentary committee on computers. There had been a special OECD exercise conducted in Norway on the subject. There was a central unit for computers and a great deal of consultation with all concerned. The concentration had not been on hardware but on the training of teachers in the comprehensive schools and the development of software over a four-year period. They now had 100 educational software programmes in collaboration with employers with whom they had defined the needs and with close Nordic co-operation. They had also developed them well for the use of the handicapped. Now they wanted to train other groups who could use them and disseminate their use. They did not want to create new inequalities through the use of high technology. They wanted to motivate girls and immigrant groups to participate in these developments.

Dr. Johnston (Australia) asked about the extent to which the general structure of employment and social security gave incentives to students. To some extent government subsidies might neutralise choices. *Mr. Bakke* replied that the Norwegian education authorities were determined to co-operate with the labour market and with industry to train young people. Firms received payment each year to accept young people for training programmes. But this was yet another issue that now required further evaluation. They accepted that there should be vocational training geared to the developing market and they hoped that the upper secondary schools would play a full part in supplying that market. There was not a high drop-out rate in the upper secondary school but the tight labour market persuaded young people to take jobs outside it and there was a general feeling that they did not work hard enough at school. In answer to *Prof. Sette*, Mr. Bakke reported that full employment was a political priority, but he did not know if it will be preserved.

Mr. Jonsson (Iceland) pointed out that the use of computers in schools would certainly change the role of the teachers. *Mr. Bakke* replied that the Royal Commission on Teacher Education would surely take note of this. *Mr. Tinsman* (United States) asked whether higher education was recruiting enough young people because so many were attracted into employment. *Mr. Ehnmark*(Sweden) noted the high proportion going into apprenticeships. What about the general education elements? *Mr. Bakke* replied that Norway was securing a 1.5 per cent increase in recruitment to higher education each year. They believed that more could be absorbed. Some areas needed to provide more student recruitment and were not willing to establish closer linkage with regional colleges. There was a demand from industry. They saw no problems about increasing the flow either in terms of the system's capacity or in terms of future employment. *Mrs. Grøndahl* added that because the number of young people was going down it was all the more important for adults to come back to higher education and requalify for the new employment tasks ahead. At the same time, there would be strong emphasis upon adult education. *Prof. O'Donoghue* remarked that there were other areas of higher education which had not been fully covered in the review but they should not be lost sight of. They included, for example, management education, and education for management in the schools.

VIII

TEACHER EDUCATION

The meeting then turned to consider the following questions posed by the examiners on teacher education:

Question 15

Are the authorities satisfied that the present structure and context of teacher education for the basic and upper secondary school are adequate? Is there an adequate connection in teacher education between theory and practice? Can better arrangements be made to relate provision for in-service training to pre-service training?

Question 16

What steps can be taken to ensure stronger recruitment for the comprehensive school and for certain subjects in the upper secondary schools?

Prof. Lundgren said that teacher education could be connected with centralisation. As decentralisation occurred in the schools surely it would be the more necessary for teacher education to become more centralised so that the national goals would be better achieved. Other demands on teacher education would arise from the new *Mønsterplan*. It was important that teachers were capable of advancing basic skills, of having an overview of newly developing knowledge and fully engaging in INSET. There was a need for good teachers who could follow these new developments. This argued for teacher education being nearer higher education. Many teacher colleges were small, isolated and specialist. *Mrs. Grøndahl* added that they were hoping that teacher training colleges would closely collaborate with schools in development work and INSET. *Mr. Bakke* replied that there was a committee looking into teacher education which would be considering these questions. He was not certain that teacher education could be regarded as "too open". Indeed, centralisation often allowed for greater openness rather than restriction. It was already thought to be too centralised and the Advisory Council on Teacher Education had been regarded as a "wet blanket". Its power had been reduced to give the institutions more freedom. They agreed that there were too many teacher training colleges which were not strong enough. They did not want to combine. But their advantages should not be dismissed too lightly. They were able to recruit teachers locally who stayed in remote areas which might be difficult otherwise to service.

Mr. Irving (New Zealand) said that there was a major review being undertaken in New Zealand on teacher education and the Norwegian problems were quite similar. There, too, it was thought that the central authority was applying too heavy a hand to teacher education. *Prof. O'Donoghue* noted how there were ambitions in teacher training colleges to establish new study programmes, including those leading to PhDs. But there were other severe problems inasmuch as teachers might go into industry but there was not enough traffic the other way. Younger teachers were leaving and leaving behind older teachers. *Mr. Bakke* reported an earlier point that it might be a good thing for teachers to be educated so that they could be flexible in seeking other employment later on. Perhaps the notion of a general basic training in teacher education should rule. *Mr. Healy* (Ireland) asked about the level of in-service training. *Mrs. Grøndahl* replied that there were problems about making sure that time would be available for in-service training. The unions had been reluctant to agree that time should be provided for in-service training within the school period.

Mr. Kjelberg of the Norwegian Ministry of Cultural and Scientific Affairs said that teachers in upper secondary schools could go to universities for both pedagogical and in-service training. There had been a deterioration of teaching because young women's opportunities had now opened up for other professions. *Mr. Bakke* (referring to Mrs. Grøndahl) remarked that some women, indeed, became Ministers of Education. That could not be a bad thing.

Mrs. Hostmark-Tarrou (Norway) described the patterns of education provided in her vocational teacher training college in Oslo. The need was for stronger training in both vocational subjects and related pedagogical training.

CONCLUDING REMARKS

In bringing the session to a close, *the Chairman* said that the Education Committee would rate high the review of Norwegian educational policy. The discussion had been interesting and pertinent to many international concerns and he again congratulated both the Norwegian authorities and the examiners on the excellence of their contributions. *Mr. Bakke*, on behalf of the Norwegian government, said that they had asked the examiners, at the beginning of their visit to Norway, to be critical. They had fully met the expectations and needs of those involved in education in Norway and he again expressed gratitude to the examiners. *Mr. Gass* (Director for Social Affairs, Manpower and Education), on behalf of the OECD, noted that the French were wont to say that they had no petrol, but they did have ideas. If a time came when the Norwegians had no oil, they would still have an education system in which they had invested very much resource and belief.

Part Three

NATIONAL POLICIES FOR EDUCATION IN NORWAY

Summary of the Background Report
prepared by the Royal Ministry of Cultural and Scientific Affairs
and the Royal Ministry of Church and Education,
Oslo, 1988.

Part Two

NATIONAL POLICIES FOR EDUCATION
IN NORWAY

Summary of the Background Report
prepared by the Royal Ministry of Cultural and Scientific Affairs
and the Royal Ministry of Church and Education
Oslo, 1986

I

COUNTRY AND PEOPLE

Norway is the fifth largest country in Europe, but with only 4.1 million inhabitants, its population density is the lowest next to Iceland. The birthrate has gone down in recent years, although less than in many other Western European countries. The total population is expected to increase somewhat into the next century.

The country is 1 500 km long, and the population is very scattered. Geographic and climatic conditions have made communication difficult. During this century, there has been a general tendency to migrate from rural areas to towns, and to some extent also from the North to the South. Maintaining a certain degree of stability in the habitation has nevertheless been a major aim of Norwegian policies all through the century.

In spite of a small Sami minority in the North, and increasing immigration in recent years, the Norwegian population is culturally fairly homogeneous. This also applies in religious matters, where 95 per cent of the population belong to the Lutheran State Church.

Economically, Norway is far into the post-industrial area, with about two-thirds of the workforce employed in the services. Manufacturing industries employ 28 per cent, and primary sectors 7-8 per cent.

Norway reached one of the highest levels in the world of GNP per capita in the postwar period. Exploitation of North Sea oil resources has added significantly to the national income in the last decade, although it has also increased the country's strong dependence upon international economic conditions. Norway has been able to maintain somewhat higher rates of growth in the GNP during the last decade than the OECD average, and unemployment has been kept at a very low level, currently about 2 per cent. Inflation has, however, been higher than the OECD average, and it still constitutes a problem. Together with unfavourable terms of trade, it has caused a major deficit in the balance of foreign trade, and the government has announced a policy of economic austerity for some years ahead, especially in terms of reduced private consumption.

Politically, Norway is divided in about 450 municipalities, which through their 150 years of existence have acquired a strong political position. They are responsible for a wide range of public activities, amounting to 10 per cent of GNP, nearly as much as the State.

The municipalities are brought together in 19 counties, which in principle are public bodies at the same level as the municipalities, but with a different set of tasks. The municipalities, for instance, are responsible for running compulsory schools, while the counties have a similar responsibility for the schools at the upper secondary level.

Norway is not only a wealthy nation, it is also a country with a fairly equal distribution of income and wealth. Class distinctions are probably less marked than in most other Western countries. It takes pride in its welfare institutions, and the maintenance of Norway as a welfare society is a stated concern of all political parties.

II

THE EDUCATION SYSTEM

The extensive use of *kindergartens* has come relatively late to Norway. The number of children in kindergartens has grown from 40 000 to 100 000 during the last decade. There is, however, still a great shortage of kindergartens, due to the high level of female participation in work outside the home, and an increasing number of single-parent families. The government has announced its intention to increase the number of kindergartens substantially, with about 5 children per adult in the institutions.

Compulsory education starts at 7 years of age, and is usually organised in a 6-year primary school and a 3-year lower secondary school. Quite often, however, the same school offers all the 9 grades. The classes are held together all through compulsory education, with no formal or informal streaming. The class teacher system is predominant, although less rigidly adhered to at the lower secondary level. Examinations and marks have been abandoned in primary education, but are regular features at the lower secondary level.

The number of compulsory schools in Norway is about 3 500, which means that the average school has about 150 pupils. The Parliament has stipulated a maximum size of a compulsory school at 450 pupils. Many schools are quite small, sometimes combining several grades in one class, in which case maximum class size is substantially reduced. Average class size in primary education is 18.5 pupils, and in lower secondary schools 23.8 pupils. Maximum class size is stipulated at 28 and 30 pupils, respectively. The pupil/teacher ratio in compulsory education is 12.5 (full-time teacher equivalents). Compulsory schools are run by the municipalities, within a framework of central government regulations, including an indicative national curriculum plan. The plan allows for considerable local variations, and also encourages local innovation activities. Some 3 000 locally initiated development projects are currently being registered.

About 90 per cent of the youngsters leaving compulsory education go on to studies at the upper secondary level. In principle, everyone has the right to 3 years of education at this level, although they may leave with a certificate after 1 or 2 years. The total number of pupils actually exceeds the size of the age group 16-18 years, as schools at this level are often attended also by young people beyond that age. In some of the most popular vocational branches of upper secondary education, some applicants are rejected, but by and large, the number of places available at this level corresponds to the number of applicants.

The *upper secondary system* offers general and vocational programmes. General programmes are now being attended by about 40 per cent of the 16-18 age group, and differentiated in a number of subject orientations. In addition, the vocational branches are also offered in a wide variety. Historically, schools for general education and vocational schools were separate, but increasingly upper secondary schools offer both general and vocational education. A policy of meeting local demand has led to the establishment of many relatively small schools, with only a limited range of courses. Many students, therefore, have to leave their homes in order to get the more specialised types of vocational training.

Although upper secondary schools are run by the counties, curriculum plans are mainly developed and introduced by central government, which also establishes the legal framework for the schools' operations.

Parallel to the vocational programmes, and largely intertwined with that system, is an apprenticeship programme recruiting by now nearly 20 per cent of the age group. The certificates obtained through apprenticeship, combined apprenticeship and school-based training, or full school-based training are equivalent.

The Ministry of Labour and Local Affairs runs extensive programme of labour market training, seen as instruments in its fight against unemployment. The courses are often organised in collaboration with educational institutions and located in such institutions. Voluntary organisations for *adult education*, often affiliated to countrywide organisations such as the trade unions, religious organisations and political parties, run a major part of adult education in Norway. Some 25 per cent of all adult Norwegians take part in an adult education course every year. The number has declined significantly in recent years, mainly due to reduced state subsidies.

Adult education at the higher education level is mostly offered by the boards of regional colleges and to some extent by the universities. Correspondence schools, operating mainly on a commercial basis, have a large clientele. Internal training activities of major private enterprises, and large branches of public utilities, also have a large number of students.

A special concern of Norwegian educational policies all through the education system is the education of the handicapped. A major programme of integrating handicapped children into ordinary compulsory schools has been in operation for more than a decade, and more than 10 per cent of all expenditures at this level are devoted to the special care of such pupils. A recent act by the Parliament gives priority to handicapped pupils for admittance to upper secondary education, and the implementation of this reform is under way. In adult education, special appropriations are given to adult education associations for the training of handicapped students. Similar measures are undertaken in higher education.

The Norwegian system of *higher education* consists of four universities, a small number of specialised institutions at university level, and about 200 smaller, usually specialised colleges, most of them organised under county-based boards of regional colleges. The latter offer courses of 2-3 years' duration, although a few institutions are also entitled to offer degrees in specific areas.

The number of students in university type institutions is 42 000, and in the colleges 51 500. In the last ten years, the total number of students in higher education has increased by 25 per cent, the strongest further increase to a total figure of 105 000 students by 1995 has been stated as the objective of government policy. The major fields of planned expansion are technology, economics, health education and teacher training. The typical age of graduation from upper secondary education in Norway is 19 years. However, most students do not enter higher education until after some years of work experience, and some interrupt their studies to achieve such experience. In addition, about 75 per cent of all young Norwegian men are drafted for twelve to fifteen months of military service. Furthermore, university studies in Norway are of relatively long duration. As a result, about 50 per cent of the student body is 25 years of age or more, and more than 20 per cent 30 years or more.

The trend towards a more heterogeneous age structure in recent years has been encouraged by the government.

Nearly 40 per cent of the 19-year-olds in Norway formally qualify for entry to higher education, but only about 25 per cent do enter. In addition, about 10 per cent of the new students are admitted on the basis of other criteria than completed upper secondary education. In most fields of study, the number of applicants exceeds the number of places available, and quantitative entry regulations are applied particularly in medicine, technology, business economics and teacher training. The regional colleges also regularly reject many applicants. On the whole, the regional colleges recruit as good students as do the universities, and students from the regional colleges also have the opportunity to continue studies at the universities.

Largely, there has been a fairly good balance between the supply of graduates from higher education and the demand of the labour market. Shortages and surpluses in specific fields have mostly been of temporary duration. Although the general dimensioning of the higher education system is somewhat geared to expected demand in the labour market, the government's policy looks primarily towards adult education, in-service training, and flexible adaptation in the economy for the adjustment of temporary imbalances in the labour market for highly-trained personnel.

The large number of small and specialised institutions of higher education causes some political concern, and the general policy of the government is to aim at some institutional consolidation. However, this runs counter to a strong tradition in Norwegian politics of using education institutions as instruments in regional development policies. This is particularly the case in the northern part of the country.

Norway spends close to 1 per cent of GNP on higher education. Budgets are felt to be very tight by the institutions, although they have mostly been saved from significant budget cuts. Even the last ten years show a certain increase in expenditures on higher education, also in terms of expenditure per student. The student/teacher ratio in the universities is 11, and 17 in the college sector.

Institutions of higher education undertake about 25 per cent of the total research and development work in Norway, and they are predominant in the field of fundamental research. The research is mainly concentrated in university-type institutions, although significant research activities have developed in some of the colleges, especially the so-called "district colleges", a kind of polytechnic institution developed over the last 20 years. The financing of research is partly funded through the university budgets, but is otherwise mainly channelled through the research councils. Private and public research contracts are increasing, but still cover probably less than 10 per cent of the total research expenditure in institutions of higher education.

For nearly 20 years, the higher education system has been developed according to reform proposals developed and adopted around 1970. The current situation is, however, characterised by uncertainty about future directions, tendencies towards defensive entrenchment within the institutions, vague attempts to become more "effective" by adopting managerial methods alien to the institutional culture, and various other forms of adaption to outside pressures. Furthermore, a period of large age groups will gradually be succeeded by a period in which youth will become scarce. The institutions of higher education may have to make themselves more attractive to the young, in view of increasing competition from both the labour market and from other channels of information, training and competence building. In view of this, the government has recently set up a Royal Commission to examine the situation of higher education and to propose directions for future policies. The Commission is expected to complete its report in the autumn of 1988.

III
SPECIAL ITEMS

In its Background Report for the OECD review, the Norwegian government has indicated a number of special items for closer scrutiny. The traditional system of *state governance* in Norwegian education could be described as a case of mild paternalism, increasingly modified over the years by local government and teacher unions.

A general tendency in recent years towards decentralisation of decision-making within the education system has led to an increase in the professional autonomy of the individual schools and institutions. To some extent, this has run counter to a more general tendency towards decentralisation of decision-making from central government to local authorities. A major step towards increasing the decision-making power of local authorities in the field of education was made in 1985, when a system of fairly detailed earmarking of grants from central government to education at the primary and secondary level was replaced by a lump-sum grant covering all central government transfers to local authorities for current expenditures. In principle, this leads to much more discretion for the municipalities and the counties in the distribution of resources between educational and other purposes. Until now, the indications are that this new system of financing has given education a greater share of local resources, although it is still too early to evaluate the results.

The teacher unions have been sceptical towards the change in government financing, as it threatens their well-established position as negotiation partners with central government. This also includes strong representation on advisory bodies to the government in the education field, as well as in central activities on curriculum development.

Other important factors in the educational field are economic organisations, particularly involved in the development of vocational training. Adult education associations, and the interest groups behind them, have a major share in running adult education. Student organisations also have a say, especially in higher education and in relation to student welfare policies.

Legal instruments play an important role in central government policies for education. General regulations on work environment, safety, buildings and other facilities also apply to education. Salaries for teachers at all levels are centrally negotiated within the framework of general salary regulations for public employees. Class size in primary and secondary education, the length of the school year, the minimum number of lessons to be offered, and teaching obligations are also centrally determined, while the size and location of schools depend on local decisions, as well as the hiring of teachers and the daily running of schools. In higher education, central government budgets provide a frame for decisions at the institutional level.

In upper secondary education, centrally determined, nationwide examinations are applied, while examination requirements in higher education are largely determined at the institutional level.

Financially, the central government plays an essential role in education, as it finances 40 per cent of compulsory education, 60 per cent of upper secondary education and 100 per cent of higher education. The rest is covered by the local authorities' own income.

Public education is offered free of charge, except in the adult education sector. Student aid is available for everybody, mostly in the form of relatively favourable loans. High interest rates in recent years have, however, caused anxiety that the student aid system is not sufficient to prevent economic factors from reducing educational ambitions for potential applicants.

The new system of lump-sum grants from central government to local authorities replaces a system based on strong "positive discrimination", to the effect that expenditure per pupil in compulsory education is on the average twice as high in rural and peripheral municipalities as in the richer, centrally-located municipalities. The result is that in terms of resources, and even outcomes, geographical differences in the quality of schooling offered have been avoided. Fears that the new financial system will lead to more unequal educational services have not yet been substantiated.

In higher education, the county-based boards of regional colleges function as administrative umbrellas for the colleges within their regions. They advise on budgetary appropriations, but decisions for each individual institution are still taken at the central level. The possibility of increasing the discretion of the boards of the regional colleges in economic and other matters is a subject for political dispute.

Private institutions are rare at the primary and secondary level in Norway. Schools serving particular religious or pedagogical purposes, or offering needed training capacity not provided by the public system, are entitled to financial support in line with corresponding public institutions. The same applies to private institutions in higher education, which have some 15 per cent of the total student body at this level. Adult education offered by countrywide voluntary associations is also entitled to public financing of a certain percentage of their expenditures.

Informative instruments play an important part in Norwegian education policy, and their importance tends to increase as the use of legal and financial instruments is modified.

Curriculum plans, largely of an indicative nature, are developed centrally for primary and secondary education. The plans usually define a core curriculum, but offer considerable leeway for local adaptations.

Norway has no inspectorate, but a system of support functions for the schools is operating at the regional and local level. Development work and school experiments are encouraged, especially in the form of local initiatives. Central research efforts have been reduced in recent years, but are now gradually being reinforced.

In higher education, central authorities exert no major influence on the curriculum of university-type institutions, but specialised Advisory Councils have some controlling and developmental functions in specific areas such as teacher training, health education and social work education.

The trend in Norwegian education policy has clearly been towards decentralisation of authority, and this seems to be the direction also for the future. Fashionable management methods in terms of stricter "evaluation", or increased external control under the label of "accountability", have not yet been widely accepted.

Teacher training is another key element in Norwegian educational policy. The basic teacher training for compulsory education is mainly located in teacher training colleges, and has a duration of 3 years. Teaching in lower secondary schools requires an additional year of training, or a corresponding degree from a university. Teachers in upper secondary education have either a full university degree of professional training in specific vocational fields with additional pedagogical training.

The problems of teacher training will be examined by a recently-appointed Royal Commission, expected to report to the government in 1988.

Equality objectives are an important concern in all fields of Norwegian politics. More equality in living conditions between social classes, geographical areas, ethnic and religious groups, etc., has since long been in the forefront of political debate and action. In recent decades, special emphasis has been put on *equality between the sexes*.

An administrative structure, including a council for equal status, an "ombudsman" function, and equality commissions within the ministries and in larger public institutions have been created. Each ministry has developed its own programme for increased equality between the sexes, as part of an overall government plan.

In education, women are now in majority in upper secondary education and among the new enrolments in higher education. Practically the whole real increase in the student body in higher education is due to an increased recruitement of women, and they now constitute 50 per cent of all students in higher education.

However, they are still in minority among the graduates from the longer studies. Among teachers, women are dominant in primary education, and constitute slightly more than 50 per cent of the total number of teachers in compulsory education. At the university level, women are not proportionally represented among the teachers, and especially not in the top positions.

Government actions to promote equality include reviewing curricula at all stages of education, encouragement for girls to enter male-dominated studies and occupations (in some cases also encouragement for men to enter female-dominated occupations), and extensive courses for women with a variety of educational backgrounds. Extensive research activities are undertaken, and a centre for "research on women and women in research" has been established under one of the research councils.

Policies for equality in terms of educational services have long traditions in Norway. Such policies aim at equal education opportunities, as well as a fair distribution of *local development* possibilities. They are reinforced by the experience that the localisation of educational institutions has major effects on local recruitment, as well as on the provision of educated manpower in the same region.

Perhaps the most outstanding example of regional concerns directing educational policies is the establishment of the University of Tromsö in northern Norway. The university has been successful in recruiting local students, and is seen as attractive for teachers from all over the country. The orientation of its research and teaching is towards regional problems, and the university has been able to establish itself as an important competence centre for development in the region as a whole.

The establishment of "district colleges" in all counties has had a similar effect. They have also formed the basis for regional research foundations, oriented towards the specific problems of the regions.

Northern Norway has a certain out-migration, which is seen as unwanted, politically, economically, socially and culturally. At the same time, this remote region has difficulties in recruiting the qualified staff needed to run its educational institutions. As an attempt to solve this problem, the region is now declared "an exceptional area" in terms of educational policy, exempt from normal central regulations. This applies to teacher salaries as well as other financial incentives, such as the partial writing off of study loans, extra grants for students and apprentices, etc. A special plan for research and development in the northern counties has also been prepared by the government.

Lifelong learning has since long been adopted as a general governing principle in Norwegian education. In 1986, a Royal Commission presented a report to the government on further steps towards the implementation of such a policy. The proposals include legislation safeguarding the right to educational leave. It also outlines a system of income maintenance during studies for people who have previously left the education system.

The report also outlines policies for changes in educational institutions in order to serve the objectives of lifelong learning, as well as for strengthening the system of adult education. The report also proposes improved mechanisms for the recognition of informal competence acquired outside the regular education system.

The proposals of the Commission have far-reaching economic consequences, which means that their implementation will have to be gradual. The government is currently studying the proposals, as a basis for the preparation of a White Paper to the Storting.

IV

SOME KEY ISSUES

The history of Norwegian educational policy after the Second World War can roughly be divided into three main phases:
Until the mid-1960s, the main political focus was on expanding the system, in order to provide *access* to education for a greatly increased proportion of the population. The next decade, while still a period of strong quantitative growth, was marked by far-reaching reforms in the *structure* of the education system. In the last decade, the main political emphasis has been on what in a wide sense could be termed the *content* of the education offered, which to a great extent amounts to a question of who controls education. Yet, in each new phase, the main problems of previous phases have still made themselves felt, making educational policies more and more complex.

Dimensioning the system

Taken as a whole, the proportion of the Norwegian population taking part in educational activities has doubled since the Second World War. The expansion of compulsory education, and the gradual realisation of the right for everyone to three years of upper secondary education, have brought participation rates for the 15-18 age group up to a very high level compared to most other countries. Higher education has also been greatly expanded although, relatively speaking, participation in formal education at this level still lags somewhat behind some of the most advanced countries. This should be seen, however, against the background of an informal adult education system engaging about one quarter of the adult population every year. Education for children below compulsory school age has also been substantially expanded, but there is still a long way to go before the demand for such education is satisfied.

In terms of further numerical expansion, pre-school education is currently in focus, with very ambitious plans presented by the government. Whether this will also imply a lowering of the compulsory school age is an open question. The present government has expressed the view that the kind of training offered in kindergartens is probably more appropriate for children below 7 years of age, but the transition from kindergartens to schools should be harmonized, which may make the distinction less meaningful.

Pupil numbers in compulsory schools are on the decline, although the reduction is not expected to be as strong as in many other Western countries. Increased time of instruction in primary schools and improved standards have up to now not made a decline in the number of active teachers possible. On the contrary, the number of teaching posts has increased significantly in the last couple of years, causing a (temporary) shortage of teachers.

At the age level of upper secondary education, the number of youngsters staying out of the school system has become rather limited, and they meet difficulties in the labour market. The trend towards increased participation is therefore likely to continue, especially in terms of prolonged vocational training. Probably, this training will increasingly take place through various forms of apprenticeship arrangements. A future decline in the relevant age groups is expected to reduce the demand for further quantitative expansion in this part of the education system.

Increased unemployment in the late 1970s caused anxiety that we would face corresponding unemployment among higher education graduates. Such unemployment has not, however, materialised to any significant extent. On the contrary, there is an obvious shortage of qualified people in a number of fields, e.g. electronic engineering, health services and teaching. The relatively restrictive policy of the 1980s in relation to higher education has, therefore, been released by a somewhat more expansionist policy, although as yet in rather cautious dimensions. Comparisons with other countries may indicate that the present policies are too cautions in this respect.

Adult education has had a certain set-back in participation, mainly due to budgetary cuts. The need for a functioning system of lifelong education may point towards increased efforts in this field in the future. This may also imply a stronger involvement by educational institutions in recurrent education, and might raise the question of some form of "open university" arrangement.

Structuring the system

There is fairly widespread agreement in Norway that the main structural features of the education system should be maintained for a considerable time-span ahead. Lowering the beginning age in primary education may be a point for debate in the years to come, but there is no serious disagreement about the maintenance of the compulsory school as a non-streamed comprehensive system.

In upper secondary education, the trend towards comprehensive schools is likely to continue, although the integration of general and vocational streams at the school level still raises considerable problems, as does the practical balancing of school-based and enterprise-based training.

In higher education, the present dual system has been fairly well integrated, and the future is likely to see a further development in this direction. Merging small, isolated institutions into more scientifically valid units is a stated policy objective, and some progress has been achieved. However, this policy runs counter to the strong tendency in Norwegian politics to see the location of educational institutions as part of policies for regional development. Resistance towards "school consolidation", at all educational levels, is strong in Norway, and not only for reasons of local policy. There may also be valid pedagogical and educational arguments for smaller units, especially where primary schools are concerned. However, it is now a fairly accepted view that in higher education the institutional atomisation of the system may have gone too far.

Adult education may be one of the areas in which structural changes could raise major political issues, relating to the division of functions between educational institutions, adult education associations and firms. The field is potentially open for new organisational initiatives.

What kind of education

In spite of its formally centralised structure, the Norwegian education system has in many respects been the domain of the teachers. Their professional ideas about what youngsters ought to know, and how they can become good and useful adults, have to a great extent shaped the real curriculum as it emerges at the classroom level. Modifications in recent years in nationwide curriculum plans and centralised examination requirements, as well as in financial regulations, have tended to strenghten the position of the individual school and the individual teacher. Yet, at the same time, interests outside the school have shown a tendency for stronger involvement in school affairs. Economic organisations are developing views on educational policies, as do professional pressure groups and ideological organisations. Parents have become more active in their attitudes and requirements towards the school, and the pupils and students themselves want to have more of a say over their education. Local political bodies want to come in between the central government and the schools, and political parties seem less prone to leave educational matters to the professional educators.

Organisational mechanisms for increased communication and shared influence have been established between the schools, the pupils, the parents, economic organisations and enterprises, and professional groups, and more decision-making power has been delegated to local authorities. However, there are also political claims for more central control of core curricula and performance indicators, such as exams.

In primary and secondary education, there seems to be unanimity that we need a strengthening of the international aspects and outlook of the curriculum, as seems logical for a small country in an increasingly integrated world. At the same time, however, a small country needs to fight for its own cultural identity, so we have all agreed that the Norwegian language and the transmission of our cultural heritage need strengthening. Furthermore, in order to cope with the modern scientific world, mathematics and natural sciences are important, as well as civics and basic technological understanding, including acquaintance with computers. On top of all this, the school is supposed to introduce youngsters to adult life, with all the problems that are involved, such as peace and international understanding, environmental issues, the fight against drugs, alcohol and tobacco, sexual behaviour, hygiene, traffic rules, etc. And out of this process should come knowledgeable and morally responsible people. Teachers feel somewhat overburdened by all those demands, and at least not appropriately rewarded in terms of pay and general respect.

At the level of higher education, the question of relevance and practical usefulness is in focus, as well as the insistence upon "quality". As "quality" must be measured in terms of what one would want the students to achieve, the term is open to widely different interpretations. It is not obvious that it should mean performance in traditional academic terms, as the debate of the 1970s has at least left some doubts about whether traditional academic ideals are sufficient as a measure of "quality".

In concrete, structural terms, this means that the eternal questions of discipline-based knowledge versus interdisciplinarity, applied versus fundamental research, the extent to which higher education institutions should be more dependent upon outside financing, etc., are constant sources of dispute. Research policy is important for academic institutions, and much of the responsibility in this field has been left with the research councils. One question is whether the larger institutions should have more financial leeway in determining their own research policies. Another is how to organise contacts between the predominant service sectors of the economy and higher education and research, to counterbalance the current sponsoring dominance by the big buyers in the sector of manufacturing industry.

The objectives

Behind all this is a set of general policy objectives, for which educational policies are among the most important instruments. We would like to promote a balanced economic development, with proper concern for the individuals involved and for the environment. We would like to see more equality between individuals, social groups and regions, both in terms of material and intellectual resources. We would like to develop democratic activities and participation for everyone in society. Cultural activities should be further developed and more widely spread, aiming at a vital and pluralistic cultural life. International understanding and peace should be promoted, emphasizing international solidarity and more equality in living conditions. And we would like to see each individual in the education system develop into mature, knowledgeable and responsible adult citizens.

At the rhetoric level, there is widespread consensus on all those points, although the practical implementation in educational terms leaves room for considerable disagreement. We have, however, come quite a long way towards opening the education system from bottom to top to everyone who wants to make use of it, and even to compensate for some of the handicaps that might prevent many from participating. Economic problems hardly block anyone from access, although more can be done to assist those with small means. No part of the education system is a definite dead end, but still more could be done to facilitate further progress within the system, and particularly the recurrent use of the system by individuals in adult phases of their life.

We are probably still emphasizing too strongly the function of the education system in selecting individuals for various positions in society, a selection which might easily run counter to essential educational goals. In doing so, we may not by far utilise the potential of children and young people to take an active part in their own education. If we succeeded better in this respect, it would probably release far more of the learning potential of adults, through a more active use of educational opportunities.

Whether the expansion of education will continue in the future, and how far, is basically dependent upon the extent to which it is seen as meeting the needs of all individuals, with their strongly varied abilities, conditions and interests. We feel that our education system still has a long way to go to meet such an objective, which requires far more than increased economic resources. Yet, through a wide range of measures, many of them outside the direct reach of educational policy, we are striving towards a continuous improvement in this direction. It is our hope that the OECD examiners will be able to provide some assistance in this struggle.

WHERE TO OBTAIN OECD PUBLICATIONS
OÙ OBTENIR LES PUBLICATIONS DE L'OCDE

Argentina – Argentine
Carlos Hirsch S.R.L.
Galeria Güemes, Florida 165, 4° Piso
1333 Buenos Aires
Tel. 30.7122, 331.1787 y 331.2391
Telegram: Hirsch-Baires
Telex: 21112 UAPE-AR. Ref. s/2901
Telefax:(1)331-1787

Australia – Australie
D.A. Book (Aust.) Pty. Ltd.
11-13 Station Street (P.O. Box 163)
Mitcham, Vic. 3132   Tel. (03)873.4411
Telex: AA37911 DA BOOK
Telefax: (03)873.5679

Austria – Autriche
OECD Publications and Information Centre
4 Simrockstrasse
5300 Bonn (Germany)   Tel. (0228)21.60.45
Telex: 8 86300 Bonn
Telefax: (0228)26.11.04
Gerold & Co.
Graben 31
Wien I   Tel. (0222)533.50.14

Belgium – Belgique
Jean De Lannoy
Avenue du Roi 202
B-1060 Bruxelles
Tel. (02)538.51.69/538.08.41
Telex: 63220

Canada
Renouf Publishing Company Ltd.
1294 Algoma Road
Ottawa, Ont. K1B 3W8   Tel. (613)741.4333
Telex: 053-4783 Telefax: (613)741.5439
Stores:
61 Sparks Street
Ottawa, Ont. K1P 5R1   Tel. (613)238.8985
211 Yonge Street
Toronto, Ont. M5B 1M4   Tel. (416)363.3171
Federal Publications
165 University Avenue
Toronto, ON M5H 3B9   Tel. (416)581.1552
Les Publications Fédérales
1185 rue de l'Université
Montréal, PQ H3B 1R7   Tel. (514)954-1633
Les Éditions La Liberté Inc.
3020 Chemin Sainte-Foy
Sainte-Foy, P.Q. G1X 3V6
Tel. (418)658.3763
Telefax: (418)658.3763

Denmark – Danemark
Munksgaard Export and Subscription Service
35, Norre Sogade, P.O. Box 2148
DK-1016 Kobenhavn K
Tel. (45 33)12.85.70
Telex: 19431 MUNKS DK
Telefax: (45 33)12.93.87

Finland – Finlande
Akateeminen Kirjakauppa
Keskuskatu 1, P.O. Box 128
00100 Heisinki   Tel. (358 0)12141
Telex: 125080 Telefax: (358 0)121.4441

France
OECD/OCDE
Mail Orders/Commandes par correspondance:
2 rue André-Pascal
75775 Paris Cedex 16   Tel. (1)45.24.82.00
Bookshop/Librairie:
33, rue Octave-Feuillet
75016 Paris   Tel. (1)45.24.81.67
(1)45.24.81.81
Telex: 620 160 OCDE
Telefax: (33-1)45.24.85.00
Librairie de l'Université
12a, rue Nazareth
13602 Aix-en-Provence   Tel. 42.26.18.08

Germany – Allemagne
OECD Publications and Information Centre
4 Simrockstrasse
5300 Bonn   Tel. (0228)21.60.45
Telex: 8 86300 Bonn
Telefax: (0228)26.11.04

Greece – Grèce
Librairie Kauffmann
28 rue du Stade
105 64 Athens   Tel. 322.21.60
Telex: 218187 LIKA Gr

Hong Kong
Government Information Services
Publications (Sales) Office
Information Service Department
No. 1 Battery Path
Central   Tel. (5)23.31.91
Telex: 802.61190

Iceland – Islande
Mal Mog Menning
Laugavegi 18, Postholf 392
121 Reykjavik   Tel. 15199/24240

India – Inde
Oxford Book and Stationery Co.
Scindia House
New Delhi 110001   Tel. 331.5896/5308
Telex: 31 61990 AM IN
Telefax: (11)332.5993
17 Park Street
Calcutta 700016   Tel. 240832

Indonesia – Indonésie
Pdii-Lipi
P.O. Box 269/JKSMG/88
Jakarta12790   Tel. 583467
Telex: 62 875

Ireland – Irlande
TDC Publishers – Library Suppliers
12 North Frederick Street
Dublin 1   Tel. 744835/749677
Telex: 33530 TDCP EI Telefax : 748416

Italy – Italie
Libreria Commissionaria Sansoni
Via Benedetto Fortini, 120/10
Casella Post. 552
50125 Firenze   Tel. (055)645415
Telex: 570466 Telefax: (39.55)641257
Via Bartolini 29
20155 Milano   Tel. 365083
La diffusione delle pubblicazioni OCSE viene assicurata dalle principali librerie ed anche da:
Editrice e Libreria Herder
Piazza Montecitorio 120
00186 Roma   Tel. 679.4628
Telex: NATEL I 621427
Libreria Hoepli
Via Hoepli 5
20121 Milano   Tel. 865446
Telex: 31.33.95 Telefax: (39.2)805.2886
Libreria Scientifica
Dott. Lucio de Biasio "Aeiou"
Via Meravigli 16
20123 Milano   Tel. 807679
Telefax: 800175

Japan – Japon
OECD Publications and Information Centre
Landic Akasaka Building
2-3-4 Akasaka, Minato-ku
Tokyo 107   Tel. 586.2016
Telefax: (81.3)584.7929

Korea – Corée
Kyobo Book Centre Co. Ltd.
P.O. Box 1658, Kwang Hwa Moon
Seoul   Tel. (REP)730.78.91
Telefax: 735.0030

Malaysia/Singapore – Malaisie/Singapour
University of Malaya Co-operative Bookshop Ltd.
P.O. Box 1127, Jalan Pantai Baru 59100
Kuala Lumpur
Malaysia   Tel. 756.5000/756.5425
Telex: 757.3661
Information Publications Pte. Ltd.
Pei-Fu Industrial Building
24 New Industrial Road No. 02-06
Singapore 1953   Tel. 283.1786/283.1798
Telefax: 284.8875

Netherlands – Pays-Bas
SDU Uitgeverij
Christoffel Plantijnstraat 2
Postbus 20014
2500 EA's-Gravenhage   Tel. (070)78.99.11
Voor bestellingen: Tel. (070)78.98.80
Telex: 32486 stdru Telefax: (070)47.63.51

New Zealand – Nouvelle-Zélande
Government Printing Office
Customer Services
P.O. Box 12-411
Freepost 10-050
Thorndon, Wellington
Tel. 0800 733-406   Telefax: 04 499-1733

Norway – Norvège
Narvesen Info Center – NIC
Bertrand Narvesens vei 2
P.O. Box 6125 Etterstad
0602 Oslo 6
Tel. (02)67.83.10/(02)68.40.20
Telex: 79668 NIC N Telefax: (47 2)68.53.47

Pakistan
Mirza Book Agency
65 Shahrah Quaid-E-Azam
Lahore 3   Tel. 66839
Telex: 44886 UBL PK. Attn: MIRZA BK

Portugal
Livraria Portugal
Rua do Carmo 70-74
1117 Lisboa Codex   Tel. 347.49.82/3/4/5

Singapore/Malaysia Singapour/Malaisie
See "Malaysia/Singapore"
Voir "Malaisie/Singapour"

Spain – Espagne
Mundi-Prensa Libros S.A.
Castello 37, Apartado 1223
Madrid 28001   Tel. (91) 431.33.99
Telex: 49370 MPLI Telefax: (91) 275.39.98
Libreria Internacional AEDOS
Consejo de Ciento 391
08009 –Barcelona   Tel. (93) 301-86-15
Telefax: (93) 317-01-41

Sweden – Suède
Fritzes Fackboksföretaget
Box 16356, S 103 27 STH
Regeringsgatan 12
DS Stockholm   Tel. (08)23.89.00
Telex: 12387 Telefax: (08)20.50.21
Subscription Agency/Abonnements:
Wennergren-Williams AB
Box 30004
104 25 Stockholm   Tel. (08)54.12.00
Telex: 19937 Telefax: (08)50.82.86

Switzerland – Suisse
OECD Publications and Information Centre
4 Simrockstrasse
5300 Bonn (Germany)   Tel. (0228)21.60.45
Telex: 8 86300 Bonn
Telefax: (0228)26.11.04
Librairie Payot
6 rue Grenus
1211 Genève 11   Tel. (022)731.89.50
Telex: 28356
Maditec S.A.
Ch. des Palettes 4
1020 Renens/Lausanne   Tel. (021)635.08.65
Telefax: (021)635.07.80
United Nations Bookshop/Librairie des Nations-Unies
Palais des Nations
1211 Genève 10
Tel. (022)734.60.11 (ext. 48.72)
Telex: 289696 (Attn: Sales)
Telefax: (022)733.98.79

Taïwan – Formose
Good Faith Worldwide Int'l. Co. Ltd.
9th Floor, No. 118, Sec. 2
Chung Hsiao E. Road
Taipei   Tel. 391.7396/391.7397
Telefax: (02) 394.9176

Thailand – Thaïlande
Suksit Siam Co. Ltd.
1715 Rama IV Road, Samyan
Bangkok 5   Tel. 251.1630

Turkey – Turquie
Kültur Yayinlari Is-Türk Ltd. Sti.
Atatürk Bulvari No. 191/Kat. 21
Kavaklidere/Ankara   Tel. 25.07.60
Dolmabahce Cad. No. 29
Besiktas/Istanbul   Tel. 160.71.88
Telex: 43482B

United Kingdom – Royaume-Uni
H.M. Stationery Office
Gen. enquiries   Tel. (01) 873 0011
Postal orders only:
P.O. Box 276, London SW8 5DT
Personal Callers HMSO Bookshop
49 High Holborn, London WC1V 6HB
Telex: 297138 Telefax: 873.8463
Branches at: Belfast, Birmingham, Bristol, Edinburgh, Manchester

United States – États-Unis
OECD Publications and Information Centre
2001 L Street N.W., Suite 700
Washington, D.C. 20036-4095
Tel. (202)785.6323
Telex: 440245 WASHINGTON D.C.
Telefax: (202)785.0350

Venezuela
Libreria del Este
Avda F. Miranda 52, Aptdo. 60337
Edificio Galipan
Caracas 106
Tel. 951.1705/951.2307/951.1297
Telegram: Libreste Caracas

Yugoslavia – Yougoslavie
Jugoslovenska Knjiga
Knez Mihajlova 2, P.O. Box 36
Beograd   Tel. 621.992
Telex: 12466 jk bgd

Orders and inquiries from countries where Distributors have not yet been appointed should be sent to: OECD Publications Service, 2 rue André-Pascal, 75775 Paris Cedex 16.
Les commandes provenant de pays où l'OCDE n'a pas encore désigné de distributeur devraient être adressées à : OCDE, Service des Publications, 2, rue André-Pascal, 75775 Paris Cedex 16.

12/89

OECD PUBLICATIONS, 2 rue André-Pascal, 75775 PARIS CEDEX 16
PRINTED IN FRANCE
(91 90 01 1) ISBN 92-64-13315-1 - No. 45041 1989